AMEN

AMEN

How **Adam Scott** won the
US Masters and broke the
curse of Augusta National

WILL SWANTON
& BRENT READ

SYDNEY • MELBOURNE • AUCKLAND • LONDON

First published in 2013

Allen & Unwin
83 Alexander Street
Crows Nest NSW 2065
Australia
Phone: (61 2) 8425 0100
Email: info@allenandunwin.com
Web: www.allenandunwin.com

Cataloguing-in-Publication details are available
from the National Library of Australia
www.trove.nla.gov.au

ISBN 978 1 74331 846 1

Internal design by Phil Campbell
Set in 12.5/18 pt Bembo by Post Pre-press Group, Australia
Printed and bound in Australia by Griffin Press

10 9 8 7 6 5 4 3 2 1

'I have observed in my lifetime
that there is always a tragedy
at that tournament.'
Peter Thomson

CONTENTS

FIRE IN THE HOLE

IF ONLY WILLPOWER AND DESIRE COULD DETERMINE WHETHER A PUTT DROPPED. Then Adam Scott would be assured of winning the US Masters. There would be some sort of supernatural recognition and reward for the endless toil and gruesome heartache that has gone into arriving at this moment and his ball would dive into the hole before shooting back out in a blaze of metaphorical fireworks. What he would give. He's a multimillionaire and yet nothing in his fattened bank account can ensure the arrival of a brand-spanking Titleist Pro V1 in its preferred resting place of tin cup—small (and getting smaller) in the gloaming.

His exquisite knack of shooting the lights out with a swing buffed enough to have its own Calvin Klein ad has earned him the widespread respect of his mostly ruthless gang of peers, all the righteous and the wicked stalking the world's pro tours, yet no shot he has ever hit (nor putting stroke he has ever unfurled) has mattered as much as this twelve-foot slider across Augusta's empire of dirt.

The dream sequence. The putt that made him whisper in boyhood. *This to win the Masters.*

Scott's reputation for being a generally nice bloke has triggered an annoying influx of sympathy towards his perceived failures at majors; according to his contemporaries and the mostly faceless scribes/jackals of the press, he is 'the greatest player never to win a major'. What a back-handed compliment, hold the compliment. What a condescending sledge. Now is his right of reply. Now comes the putt he has craved all his life. Darkness falls. Confetti rain. Be courageous! Fear nothing and fear everything. Augusta will spit in his face if it decides he is unworthy. *Are you worthy? Do you really believe that?* Augusta will hurl him into Rae's Creek with the rest of the crushed souls who blinked at the death. Witches cackle. Because for every heroic moment embroidered into the loaded history of one of the most prodigious sporting events on earth, tragedy has reared its somewhat Shakespearean head in equal measure. 'Tis the beauty of the place, the blessing and the curse. It is everything Scott ever wanted. The haloes and the blood.

In Florida, Greg Norman, one of the few to keep the faith when Scott was unable to differentiate between his arse and his elbow in 2009, has a tear in his eye from the utter gut-wrenching torment of placing an emotional investment in a golfer trying to navigate his way around Amen Corner and beyond. Only now does Norman understand the impact he had on the rest of us. Norman is painted as the motivational architect of Scott's triumphs, but please . . . some perspective. Sixty yards from the 10th green, standing under a tree, is the real inspiration. The man who really has travelled all roads. His father, Phil, can barely breathe. *This to win the Masters.*

And then Scott rests the fingertips of his trembling right hand on his Hills Hoist/winged keel of a putter. *This to win the Masters.* And then he crouches as if peering down a periscope. And then his elbows lock into place like he's about to start strumming Bach's Cello Suite No. 1. And then comes his moment of truth. The stroke is crisp and assured. *Clink.* That's always the sound of a putt. *Clink.* And then in a silence so complete he can actually hear it, a silence so eerily fulsome and thick that time grinds to a halt while Augusta's bothersome gods contemplate if Adam Scott should be constantly ignored or remembered always, slowly his ball rolls towards oblivion or the hole.

1

THE CURSE OF AUGUSTA

'People use the word choke, but I don't think that's right. I just plain screwed up.'
Greg Norman

On Gate A off Berckmans Road is a list of the prohibitions for the 77th instalment of the US Masters. No sitting in the standing areas. No standing in the sitting areas. No cameras. No hats worn backwards. Bart! No metal golf spikes. No large hats. No carts. No lying down. No sleeping. No ladders. No recorders. No periscopes. No running. No bare feet. No folding chairs. No flags. No signs. No banners. No coolers. No strollers. No radios. No cell phones. No selling of tickets/badges within

2700 feet of an Augusta gate. If you have to ask, the answer is no. So don't ask. Posture! Close your mouth when you eat.

The main entrance along Washington Road displays a genteel enough pronouncement of the name of the premises, Augusta National Golf Club, followed by a stern and imposing reminder of the preferred clientele: MEMBERS ONLY. For one week only, the riffraff are allowed through the venerable gates if in possession of the hottest and most exclusive ticket in sport. Magnolia Lane is the 330-yard roadway that made Lee Trevino's car choke. Sixty-one Magnolia trees framed the tar, planted before the Civil War, until one of them was fried by a bolt of lightning during a severe thunderstorm in 2011. The trees' branches meet overhead, creating a tunnel effect. Augusta's clubhouse is a relic from the 1930s that would have been levelled and replaced by a more elaborate construction if the green-coated gentlemen of the south had any cash during the Great Depression. Augusta's membership in a state of financial disrepair: the horror of it all.

A plaque honours the first and most influential chairman, Clifford Roberts, the founder of the tournament in 1934 with the revered American player, Bobby Jones. Diagnosed with terminal cancer in old age, Roberts had a haircut from the clubhouse barber, left a note for his wife with a doctor's report, walked down near the par-three course about 3 a.m. and shot himself in the head with a Smith and Wesson .38. Legend states that he did it next to a pond so the mess would be easiest to clean up. Dedicated to the impossible pursuit of perfection, the creator of a golfing nirvana where every blade of grass seems to have its own name, Roberts was no longer perfect enough himself. His body was found at 8 a.m. His ashes would be scattered across the course. 'From the time I met Clifford Roberts until his death, I never knew him to do anything that was not in the best interest of Augusta National,' says Jack Nicklaus. The late Sam Snead, however, was among the many conspiracy theorists: 'The caddies think his death was a murder, not a suicide, and I believe them.'

What an unusual place it is. Adam Scott is making his 12th appearance on this big, sprawling colossus of a course. The layout is extraordinarily difficult. The pin placement on the Masters *logo* is tough: front and right. Scott's prior attempts have provided all the snapshots of unfulfilled ambition: the frustrations, the near misses, the blowouts and yet the nagging, crucial understanding that you only have to win it once. Scott has monstered the par fives in a combined 57 under since his debut in 2002. But he's been humbled and beaten by the par fours: 63 over.

For eleven straight years he has taken his medicine with superb Australian players of his generation, led by Stuart Appleby, Robert Allenby, Aaron Baddeley, Craig Parry and Geoff Ogilvy, all of them falling short of securing the fabled green jacket. Before them, Bruce Crampton, Peter Thomson, Jack Newton and Greg Norman felt the familiar sting of defeat. Steve Elkington, Greg Chalmers, Peter Lonard—41 Australians have launched unsuccessful missions: Norman Von Nida, Kel Nagle, David Graham, Craig Parry . . . Graham is now a member of Augusta's pin-placement squad. The ruthless bastard.

Medicine never tastes any good. Sometimes Australians have shot themselves in the foot. Sometimes they have been plumb out of luck. Greg Norman rattled off three straight 68s in 1995 but American Ben Crenshaw, high on the misery and inspiration from the death of his coach Harvey Penick, ambushed him with the tournament of his life. Winners have been as popular as Crenshaw or as lonesome as Vijay Singh, the polarising Fijian who grabbed his one and only Masters and declared on his way out the door: 'Kiss my arse, everybody.' His name was on an honour board decorated by the most famous champions: Jack Nicklaus, Arnold Palmer, Gary Player, Tom Watson, Ben Hogan, Byron Nelson, Sam Snead, Seve Ballesteros, all the behemoths. And the wildcards in Charl Schwartzel, Bubba Watson, Trevor Immelman and Zach Johnson. In 1982, Craig 'The Walrus' Stadler shocked even himself. 'Somewhere in those first one to four weeks that followed, it hit me,' says Stadler. 'I can't remember the exact moment but I'm sure I was laying in bed. And I thought, "My God, I did win that sucker."'

There is only one prohibition missing from the sign on Gate A off Berckmans Road: No Australian winners.

••●••

'If ever someone should have won a golf tournament, it was Greg Norman at the Masters,' says Jack

Newton. 'He seemed to find a way to get beat every time, apart from when what's-his-name chipped in. He got skunked there, but he should have already beaten Jack Nicklaus in '86. Jack shot an unbelievable back nine, but Greg was leading and dealing. On 18, he's tried to play a cut. Norman couldn't cut the green then, not with his irons. He shanked it out near the scoreboard and ended up taking five for Jack to win outright.

'Another year, I can't remember when exactly, he had it by the balls until he hooked it into the trees on 10 and took six. The year Nick Faldo beat him, I don't know what was happening there. He played so well those first three days. If you said to him, "Want to back yourself for a million dollars to shoot 72 or better in this last round?", I'm sure he would have taken it. But that's what can happen at Augusta. If you get off on the wrong foot on the last day, the front nine can stuff you right over. When the birdie holes come along, those par fives on the back, you're already out of business. It's too late and that's what happened to Norman against Faldo.

'If ever he was going to win a major in America, the Masters was deadset where it was going to happen. He had to win it. He's probably the best driver the game has ever seen for his length and accuracy. He hit his irons very high, which is perfect for Augusta to check the ball when the greens get firm and hard. Norman missing out wasn't a curse. It was his frailty under the pump to get the job done.'

··●··

No Luck: Newton was trumped by Seve Ballesteros in 1980. 'I was nine behind with nine to play,' he recalls. 'We were playing together, and I got it back to three. When he hooked it into the trees on 14, I thought I really had a chance. Well, I knew I had a chance. Seve and I were good friends from playing together in Europe, and I knew exactly what he was saying. He used to ask me to watch him hit balls, so I knew all the swear words he used in Spanish. He was letting it rip on the back nine. I really did think he was gone. He hit it in the water on 11. Hit in the water on 12. Hit it in the water on 13. I went birdie, birdie, birdie.

'On 14, the ball normally drops straight down if you hit one of the pine trees. It's pot luck whether you're up against the tree or not. Seve must have hit a branch because the ball went to the left. It went just far enough for him to hit it over the trees. Only Seve could have done that. He was a miracle man from trouble. He got it up and down and then on the par five, the 15th, we both had birdie putts. Mine was downhill. His was below the hole. I thought I needed to make mine, so I gave it a run. It hit the hole, spun out and went another metre past. That was it.

'To be honest, I was pleased for Seve because we were good mates, he played great and I thought he deserved it. Ironically enough, my second year at Augusta had been Seve's first. He was eighteen, nineteen, something like that. I had a good second round and in the press conference, one of the Yankee journos said to me, "Have you seen much of this Bally-a, Bally-a . . . what's his name?" And I said, "Mate, you'd better learn how to say it and spell it because you're going to be saying it and spelling it for a long time to come." When Seve beat me, and I'd done all the TV interviews, that same journo came up to me and said, "Remember the day you told me to learn how to say and spell Ballesteros? You were right."'

•• ● ••

The No Luck Club: Five Australian runners-up. The late Jim Ferrier in 1950. Bruce Crampton in 1972. 'Let me put it this way—when I was playing tournament golf I knew if I made less mistakes than everybody else, I would win the tournament,' says Crampton. 'My objective was to minimise the number of mistakes for the four tournament rounds. I think it's safe to say that from all the Australians who came close at Augusta, we collectively made one, two or three too many mistakes each. But my attitude is one of pride. In my own small way, I feel like I contributed to the success of golf in Australia with what I did. I helped to encourage some of the younger players, if not all of them, to come to the United States and test their talents over here.'

Newton in 1980. 'Augusta is not much of a town,' he says. 'But the golf course is pristine. As it ought to be. They have something like 48 staff there. About 23 of them work purely on the gardens and flowers. The rest do the greens and fairways. Their belief is that they're leading the world in golf course care, and it shows. When you drive down Magnolia Lane, you have two practice fairways and the big southern-style clubhouse in the background, it really does have an amazing feel. Everything is green and white. The television towers are painted green. If you buy a Coke, you get it in an Augusta paper cup, green and white. No cans. Everything is branded "Augusta". They sell a shitload of gear.

'I'm telling you, it's just an unbelievable set-up. For a pro golfer, it's a dream to be there. The food is great. They have some of the best red wine in the world. It's all about the prestige and the green jacket, which means you're not allowed to mention prizemoney. They used to have blokes listening to what the players said on television in case the money was mentioned. That's just the way they run it. The events you enjoy are the ones where they look after you. They're always the ones you want to go back to and for me, Augusta was always one of them. It's the duck's nuts.'

Newton's first trek was in 1976. 'The invitation comes in the mail,' he says. 'It's right there on the Augusta National letterhead. I actually thought I should have been invited the year before. By '76 I'd won a couple of tournaments in Europe and lost to Tom Watson in a playoff at the British Open. I played shit that first year. I wore a new pair of shoes, like an imbecile. I thought it's Augusta and I should wear some good gear. That's the kind of hype you feel about the place. The course itself is almost too perfect to sum up. I drove up there for the first time, went through the wrought-iron gates and went to see Clifford Roberts so he could give me a lecture of what I could and could not do. It was full-on invitational in those days. No world rankings or all the different ways they have now of qualifying. I went to see Clifford and he could have been Norman von Nida: a short little fella with horn-rimmed glasses. He was a rough, tough little guy.

'I'd come from Africa and was playing super. But I did something to my foot looking for a guy's ball. Then I wore the new shoes and had blisters from arsehole to breakfast time. Absolutely I was overawed, and I missed the cut. There was a fella who used to be the boss of the Wills company, and he always had a party for the Australians after the cut on the Friday. All the Aussies would go, and Clifford Roberts' personal assistant was always there. She was a little old sheila with plenty to say. She heard I had blisters and problems with my foot, and she must have told Clifford Roberts because next thing I know, I was being called into his office. I'm thinking bloody hell, what have I done? He said, "Listen, Jack, I understand you played under duress this year". Blah-blah-blah. He said, "You didn't come in here whinging about it, and I like that. So consider yourself invited for next year". I played every year up until '82.'

When it came to naming his sprawling house and property in Newcastle, Australia, Newton would settle on Augusta. He played five Masters before losing his right eye and arm in an altercation with the blades of a Cessna aeroplane in 1983. He returned as the sharpest commentator in Australian golf.

'First year, they make you play with an old prick,' he says. 'I can't even think of who I got. He was just an old prick who shouldn't have been playing at all. But over the years I played with a lot of good golfers there. It's a quality course that makes you think about every shot. You need to hold your nerve on the greens because they get bloody quick. When you play a practice round, you think you can make a seriously low number on the back nine if you get it going, but once the bell rings and there's a bit of breeze around holes like 11, and 12 in particular, it becomes very difficult to get the right club in your hand. The wind is swirling around those pine trees. It's just a very unusual golf course. No one ever talks about the front nine but if you don't birdie the second and possibly the third holes, it's going to be no snack for the rest of the day. You start dropping shots pretty quickly if you're not on the ball straight out of the box.

'I led in '77 or '78 after three rounds. Maybe I was equal leader? I played with Billy Kratzert, who was a hot player back then. Out of nowhere, the wind started blowing in a totally different direction to what I'd seen before. It was a strong fucking wind. It can be a bastard of a course in that kind of weather and I shot 76 or 77 and lost. It blew like buggery and I couldn't pick up the club. The whole strategy, the whole way the course played, was different. I remember it was howling into my face, from my right, on the first tee. It was a monster of an opening hole then with the equipment we were playing with. It was a tough starting hole for us. You have to have your game at a very high pitch or you're not going to win a Masters. Some of these blokes in the media think that majors are thrown on the ground and it's just a matter of picking them up, but they're bloody hard.'

•• • ••

The No Luck Club: Norman was president, elected unopposed, denied his green jacket for 22 straight years from 1981 to 2002. And then for one more year in 2009. He remembers a deep love for the game of golf washing over him on the first tee on debut. His opening round was a speckless 69 and the *Augusta Chronicle* made the rather ingenious decision to christen him the Great White Shark. Drama proceeded to shadow him around every turn. Nine top-ten finishes. Thrice a runner-up. The unfathomable yet fleeting highs. The lows.

The Norman Conquest of 1986. Full pomp and regalia! The perfect storm of charisma, bravado and whiplash skill. Norman birdied the 16th to trail Jack Nicklaus by two. The swagger! The lasso swing. The roar when Norman charged after his ball as soon as he struck it. He had a twelve-footer for birdie on 17. The pre-putt routine held as much magnetism as the stroke itself. The circling of the ball and hole. The squint. Norman was running at the cup with his blade raised like a flag before the putt even went in. He had the flourish of a swordsman. Four straight birdies to be level with Jack.

'He just jerks at his glove, tugs at his trouser belt and starts walking fast,' the caddie Nathaniel 'Iron

Man' Avery once said of Arnold Palmer. 'When Mr Palmer does that, everybody better watch out. He's going to stampede anything in his way.' Ditto for Norman, we thought. He grabbed his 3-wood. Steel shafts! Rolled his shoulders. The necessity of the fade. The absolute imperative of steering clear of the fairway bunkers on 18. Norman swung out of his shoes. Nailed it. A Norman charge was like few others. He would birdie the last and leap Butler Cabin in a single bound. Then, a deep breath. A check of the yardages. The first moment of pause. Uh-oh. Give Norman one career mulligan and he would return to this moment.

He had 180 metres to the pin. Halfway between a 4-iron and a 5-iron. Uncertain terrain. Only a golfer knows the hesitant feeling. Hammer the 5? Baby the 4? The latter would be difficult with oceans of adrenaline. He chose his weapon: the 4. His caddie said as authoritatively as possible: 'It's the perfect club.' It needed the perfect swing. The hips escaped. The club face decelerated. The ball leaked to the right. Norman's panicking eyes. His head fell to his chest. A bump-and-run down the hill. Get close. Not close enough. A putt for a playoff. Downhill and left to right. Always the hardest putt. It stayed left, missed. Nicklaus had his sixth green jacket.

The Norman Conquest of 1987. What the hell was Larry Mize doing in a playoff? Mize grabbed a sand wedge. Interrupted destiny. He took seven paces towards the 11th green. To Norman's delight, Ballesteros had been eliminated on the first playoff hole. Mize picked his landing area, the size of a dime. Such a compact and traditional stance. An abbreviated swing. Textbook. One last look at the pin. The bunt. Perfect! The rest would be a mystery. Anything can happen to a bunt, good and bad. Ball in motion. Two bounces onto the green, rolling, rolling. Great line. Great pace. Now the hype built. Look at Mize. Unmoved. Always the tell. How's it looking? How is this looking now! In the hole. Mize threw his club in the way Julia Roberts might have flung her wedding bouquet. The back-arched leap. His white visor flew off. He clapped and ran and skipped to retrieve his ball from the white cup. He held it up. Exhibit A, your honour. The collective gasp.

Norman's hand was on his waist. He glared at the green. He glared at Augusta itself. What did you just do? In that moment, Norman saw his future.

AMEN

Mize raised both palms in a request for quiet. Then his hands went down. Up again! Down. Norman fell to his haunches. His lips were pursed. He appeared to have shrunk. There was disbelief and dread. For all the machismo attached to belting drives to Kingdom Come, the nuances matter most in golf, especially at Augusta. The delicacies and touch. Norman was lost. Sport as life: the impermanence of dominance. He putted without belief. It was the stroke that never happened. On the Sunshine Coast of Australia, a six-year-old Adam Scott began to cry. Norman's poster was hanging clichéd on his bedroom wall. Norman trudged to the clubhouse. Defeat was always a silent and lonely old thing.

The Norman Conquest of '96. Inconceivable in '86 was the notion that Norman would be jacketless a decade later. Entrenched in Australia was the pastime of setting alarm clocks for 6 a.m. to watch The Shark tackle the back nine on what, at home, was a Monday morning. He was the world No. 1 for six years. Twice he won the British Open. This was the year he would receive Augusta's blessing. A course-record 63 on the opening day, mocking the course that previously belittled him. A six-shot lead from Nick Faldo for the final round. Deliverance!

He wore the Greg Norman brand of slacks. The Greg Norman brand of polo. The Greg Norman brand of wide-brimmed hat. Past heartaches and disasters would add to the enormousness of the imminent achievement. Blue skies! Translucent 65s. He could do it in style, but a 72 would do. One more lap to the chequered flag.

Norman walked across the concrete path outside the clubhouse, past Eisenhower Tree and chewed his nails. Another moment of pause. Never a promising sign. Faldo emerged from the Champions Locker Room. They shook hands and according to Faldo, Norman was unable to look him in the eye. Got him. 'I didn't think it was impossible,' recalls the Englishman. 'You think that anything can happen at Augusta. It's a very difficult tournament to lead. It's such a "feel" golf tournament and if you get nervous, your feel starts to go. I thought if I get through nine holes and I've knocked two or three shots off—three back with nine to play means nothing at Augusta.'

Norman bogeyed the first. Five the difference. Faldo birdied the sixth. Four the difference. Faldo birdied the eighth. Three the difference. Norman attacked the ninth pin. His approach dragged off the front of the green, wheels spinning. Two the difference. A clunking, ham-fisted chip at the 10th. One the difference. Norman missed a short putt at the 11th (the rotten old 11th) and it was all square. Never in Faldo's wildest dreams. Norman's tee shot at 12 drowned in Rae's Creek.

Standing on the 13th fairway, contemplating the merits of laying up or going for broke, Faldo was two strokes ahead. He leaned against his bag with the nonchalance of a man wearing coat and tie. The ball is always above a right-hander's feet on 13. Faldo was ready to lay up with a 5-wood. He hurried towards his caddie, Fanny Sunesson. 'I said to Fanny, "I want to go for it,"' says Faldo. '"I don't want to lay up." I said to her, "Well, it's a 2-iron." So I stood up and hit the thing.' He drilled the thing. He birdied 13 and 15, the commandments of Amen Corner.

Norman nearly chipped in for eagle on the 15th. What would have happened if that crisp little number had gone in? If only we knew, saints, if only we knew. Then came a defining image: Norman falling to his knees, and then onto his back, his putter/sword jammed into his stomach as though performing harakiri. The torment. Why him? No one respected the Masters more than Norman. His tee shot on 16 was pulled left. Splash. CBS's Peter Kostis told 150 million TV viewers: 'That's curtains.'

'I stood there and thought, "I don't believe it,"' says Faldo. He hugged Norman on the 18th green. Slapped his back. Norman pecked Sunesson on the cheek and scribbled his signature on a 76. Before the round, English golf writer Peter Dobereiner had sidled up to Norman at the urinal and declared: 'Not even you could fuck this one up, Greg.' It was the beginning of the drudgery. Where was the sacred kiss? 'I genuinely felt for the guy,' says Faldo. 'I mean, if it happened to me, if I was six shots up and lost a major, I would be scarred. I've won majors and I've lost majors but fortunately, I don't have any scars from them. He handled it better than anyone else probably could have handled the situation. It was a genuinely competitive day. I was looking after my camp. He was in his camp. I shot 67 and finished the week twelve under. That's the bottom line in golf. We know where the start of the race is and we know the finishing line. I hope I'm remembered for shooting a 67 on the last day, and not for what happened to Greg. But obviously this will be remembered for what happened to Greg.'

AMEN

To paraphrase Norman's comments to the bastards awaiting him, their pens dipped in ink: 'Nick's gone way up in my estimation . . . it's not the end of the world . . . I let this one get away. I'll wake up still breathing, I hope . . . I played like shit. That's probably the best way of putting it. I really got a good old ass whipping. I put all the blame on myself. I made a lot of mistakes. My swing was out of sync, my putting was out of sync. My thought pattern was good but my rhythm was out . . . Nick played great golf and I played poor . . . There's not a whole lot of anguish. My life is pretty good. I'm happy. I've got pretty good control over the situation. It's not the end of my world. I'll enjoy my life, I'm very philosophical about it. You learn and you try to understand why and what happened. I may not want to learn about this one. Maybe I just screwed up bad enough with my own mistakes . . . I've seen what the game gives you and what it takes from you. Maybe these hiccups that I inflict on myself are meant for another reason. I don't know. There must be a reason. I think there's something waiting for me down the line that's going to be good for me. My life's not over yet. Something good is going to happen before my career is over. I really believe that. All of this is just a test. I'm a winner, I just didn't win here. I'm not a loser in life. I'm not a loser in golf tournaments. I'm a perfectionist. If I wanted to be a brain surgeon I could.' He's just made $US 40 million from shares in the golf club company, Cobra. 'You see, there's a good thing about life,' he says. 'I've got something that other people haven't got. I've got 40 million bucks. God, I'd love to be putting the green jacket on. I'm sad about it, I'm going to regret it but it's not the end of the world for me.' Forty-mill can cure a few ills. No amount of legal tender, however, can ever buy Norman a green jacket.

The Norman Conquest of 1999. Stop it. More teasing. He was equal leader with Jose Maria Olazabal after 11 on Sunday. He eagled 13. 'I was in Vegas watching with my dad,' says Adam Scott. 'I jumped off the couch and thought this was the one. But then Olazabal rolled it in on top of him.' Norman three-putted the 14th and Olazabal was home. When Norman laid up on 15, a relatively simple wedge dive-bombed into the sand. That was it. All over. He finished third and never threatened again.

Seven years after what was assumed to be the dying of the light, he qualified for one last shot in

2009. Mick Jagger was back on stage. The Eagles had reunited. Norman's last unedifying duty was signing off for a 77 that assured he missed the cut. Such an unsatisfactory ending. He drove back down Magnolia Lane on a Friday night and that was it. Did he have any idea of what he meant to us all these years? 'I never thought about it,' he says. 'You're there doing a job, and that job is to play golf. If I was worried about what everybody else was doing or thinking back in Australia, I would never have been in the position to contend. I knew there was support, of course I did. But I couldn't allow myself to think about it.'

··•··

Norman provides his own compelling analysis under the headline of 'No Jacket Required'. 'I love the Masters,' he writes. 'Even though I've never won it, it is still my favourite tournament. I don't think there is an event anywhere that has brought me more enjoyment or shaped my development more profoundly as a player and, more importantly, as a person. But yes, Augusta National has been a cruel temptress to me. I've been close enough to taste victory there many times, and while I have suffered a number of heartbreaking defeats, I can honestly say I probably got more out of the tournament than anybody besides Jack Nicklaus. The Masters is pure golf. The club and the tournament are run with discipline and control, two attributes I respect. When you walk onto the first tee, you feel an overwhelming love for the game. It is the most beautiful expanse of grass you will see in the world. And the sense of history is powerful: I have really enjoyed walking in the footsteps of so many great players. I think part of my problem was that I got too excited every year. The other majors come so quickly that you never have time to worry about them. But I would start thinking about Augusta on January 1, so by the time April arrived I was already impatient. Every year has been special to me, but these in particular stand out.

'1981: I'll never forget how Augusta National struck me when I first saw it. In only my second major championship on American soil, I opened with a 69 and had a share of the lead. The media immediately started asking questions about this unknown, aggressive blond-haired Aussie who used to swim and dive with sharks. In that Friday's *Augusta Chronicle*, in large type on the cover of the sports section, the headline read: "Great White Shark Leads Masters". By Sunday I was just two shots behind Tom Watson with nine to play, but my tee shot on 10 drifted left. I chipped out, made double bogey and just couldn't recover, finishing fourth behind Watson, Nicklaus and Johnny Miller. It was a magical start to my Masters ride, and 21 consecutive such rides were to follow.

'1986: My greatest regret in golf came five years later on the 72nd hole. That was the year Nicklaus mounted his fabulous final-round charge. He started four shots behind and closed with a 65, holding the clubhouse lead for ages. After birdies on 14, 15, 16 and 17, I needed just a par on 18 to force a playoff. I was in the middle of the fairway, 187 yards out, right between a 4-iron and a 5-iron. I chose a soft 4. Wrong choice. I should have stayed in attack mode and hit the hard 5. Alas, I made bogey and handed victory to Nicklaus. If I could have one career mulligan, I'd take it there. Painful as it was, I waited around for Jack to finish with his interviews. Even though he already had five green jackets, I knew how special that moment was to him. I wanted to offer my congratulations in person—and he did the same for me at Turnberry later that year when I won my first major. He was the first to congratulate me after my caddie and my wife.

'1987: Bob Tway holing out from the bunker at the 1986 PGA Championship at Inverness, I could live with. Robert Gamez and David Frost holing out from the fairway to beat me at the 1990 Nestlé Invitational and the 1994 Greater Hartford Open, respectively—those hurt, but I got over them. The one that killed me inside was Larry Mize's pitch on the second playoff hole at the Masters in 1987. That was destiny saying, You aren't going to win this tournament. That one really rocked me.

'1996: The best four rounds I've ever put together were during the 1994 Players Championship, where I shot 264. But I came close to matching it for 54 holes at the '96 Masters. It started in the first round when I equalled Nick Price's course-record 63. My lead swelled to six shots after three rounds, and then everything started to cave in. I've never been one to shy away from my own screw-ups, and screw up is exactly what I did during that final round. People use the word "choke", but I don't think that's right. I just plain screwed up. I'd do anything to have the round over. No way would I ever shoot 78 again. I sensed early on that things weren't right. I said to Tony Navarro, my caddie, "Boy, it's going to be a tough day." I just couldn't feel what I had the previous three days. The more I tried, the more it went away. Obviously I wasn't playing well that day, but if I could take one of those 78 shots over it would be my approach to the ninth green. You have to be so precise at Augusta, and when my wedge came up three feet short and the ball rolled down the hill I knew then that the back side would be one of the longest nines I would ever play. The embrace I shared with Nick Faldo on the 18th green meant a great deal to me. He was genuinely concerned about how I would handle what happened that day, and how others would handle it. As we hugged, he leaned in and said sincerely and succinctly, "Don't let the bastards get you down." That, I'll never forget.

'Since '96, of everything that has transpired in my career, I am most proud of how I handled that loss. As devastating as it was at the time, it was important for me to go to the media centre and handle the bullets that were fired at me, and then get up, walk away and say, "Hey, it's over and done with". Too many athletes turn down the media and, in doing so, eschew their responsibilities. You need to accept what happened. When we got back home, my wife, Laura, and I went to the beach and had a good cry, which is exactly what I needed to do. I'm not one of those macho guys who think men can't cry. If you're hurting, unload. The whole experience changed my life.

'Honestly, if you had told me twenty years ago that I'd never win a green jacket, I wouldn't have believed it. Hell, after 1981 I thought I'd win one the very next year. But you can't control what other players do out there, only what you do. If you have a weakness, you have to deal with it and still get around. That is the beauty of sport. You have to know you are going to hit highs and lows. You just have to embrace your mistakes and learn from them. And I can sincerely say I have learned more about myself and my love for golf through the hard knocks than through the easy wins. I would not have the same depth of understanding if I didn't have to deal with the heartache. Sure, I would have loved to win more, but at the end of the day I didn't, and I had to channel that frustration and learn from every defeat. Ultimately it doesn't matter how many majors you've won. It doesn't matter if you've never won a single tournament. It's the commitment you make to yourself and to the game that is the measure of how great you are. I've felt agony and ecstasy. I've experienced things that very few people ever will. The days you cry your eyes out and the days you celebrate with your friends— to me, that's what it's all about. Sure, there's a part of me that feels hollow, but that feeling is part of who I have become because of the Masters, and I would not dream of trading that, even for a green jacket.'

..●..

We suggest Augusta should make Norman a member. 'Oh!' he grins. 'I don't know about that'. He's blushing crimson. A ferry is whisking him from Great Keppel Island to Rockhampton in Queensland.

'Augusta?' he repeats as though the name might ring a bell. 'Listen, I like the institution. I like the way the tournament is conducted. It's pure golf. It's clean. Some people hate it. A lot of players really don't like it but Augusta is Augusta. There are no surprises. No one is being forced to go there and play. No one has a gun to your head. Clearly, the type of club they built has worked. They do a great job in developing the game of golf. How can it be described as elitism when amateurs are allowed? When they're allowed to stay on the course itself? They grow the game worldwide. The young Chinese kid, Tianlang Guan, he's come through because of the Masters' involvement in the Asian junior program. The club does great things for our sport. You're asking me how I feel about Augusta? Well, I have always liked the tournament, and I have always liked the course. It's very easy for me to sit here and be pro-Augusta. I had a good run at it. My record there—it is what it is.'

·· ● ··

Adam Scott and Jason Day are the clubhouse leaders in 2011. Eureka! South Africa's Charl Schwartzel birdies the last four holes to win. Cursed.

Peter Thomson is a five-time British Open champion. At Augusta, his best is fifth in 1957. 'I have observed in my lifetime that there is always a tragedy at that tournament,' says Thomson. 'Somebody always loses it. Every other tournament I can think of, it's always won by someone. Augusta is always lost. It's the effect of those second nine holes. You have to really take a risk on most of them. We played with the old golf balls that didn't go the distance they do now. Amen Corner was formidable. Nobody was ever guilty of getting on the green in two on the par fives. No one could hit the ball that far when I played. You played to the corner, hit one up short of the water and then pitched it on. That's the way we played. I can remember being a bit scared of those water shots. We played conservatively in those times. Nobody was man enough to attack, but I enjoyed myself at the Masters and played well at times. I had a great reverence for Sam Snead and Ben Hogan and players like that and thought they deserved to win it, not me.'

No regrets. Except this: 'There was an ancient hotel called the BelAir with leaking plumbing and all these things', says Thomson. 'In the middle of the night, a burglar went through all the rooms and took all the wallets that people had left sitting beside their beds. The accommodation dominated our thoughts because it was so dilapidated. I braved it but everyone's notion of it was, why do we come to this place with such God-forsaken accommodation? To this day, it riles me that that happened to us.'

Cursed? 'That's a myth,' reckons Newton. 'There's no such thing.'

Scott and Day have both attended Kooralbyn International School on the Gold Coast. After his third and final year, Scott lists the following in his year book:

AMBITION: 'To be the best professional golfer in the world.'
FAVOURITE EXPRESSION: 'If all else fails, birdie the last.'
FINAL COMMENT: 'I am Adam Scott.'

2

SPOILED AND UNSPOILED WALKS

'I had to look down this year and be really honest with myself and say: "How much do you want this?"'
Adam Scott

Adam Scott grabs his first golf stick at the age of two. The little fellow progresses to clipping the ball around a par-three course near the family's home in the South Australian capital, Adelaide. They move to the Sunshine Coast when his father, Phil, receives the club professional's job at Twin Waters.

'I remember playing North Adelaide golf course with Dad,' says Scott. 'I know there are photos around of me as a two-year-old swinging a golf club, but I just remember being four or five and playing the par three . . . I was about twelve when I started playing pretty well. I was playing all the time and other sports started dropping off. Around twelve, I thought this is what I want to do with my life. I was really driven as a teenager because I seem to remember practising a lot and always being at the range. I definitely wasn't pushed, but I think I was encouraged by Dad to do that. It was so easy for me to go to the course and I probably had the passion for it.

'But you know, I used to be a real couch potato as a kid. I used to hang on the couch and do nothing. If I spent the day sitting around watching television, Dad would say, well, there's another day it's going to take for you to make it. Dad was good. Some days, I'd think about what he said. Instead of sitting on a couch for the whole week, I'd go and practise'.

Scott makes the regulation ascension. He is a two-time holder of the Australian junior title. The world junior champion at seventeen. He receives a mountain of offers to enter the US collegiate system, taking off to the University of Nevada for studies in political science while honing his Mona Lisa of a swing. Eighteen months are spent under the watchful eye of Butch Harmon. Scott's first showdown with

Harmon's student of greatest import, Tiger Woods, comes at the Rio Secco course in Las Vegas. He is given a mauling. Dormitory life is losing its lustre by now and Scott kisses Vegas goodbye to tackle the dog-eat-dog world of professionalism.

'I felt like I wasn't really moving forward,' he says. 'I always tried to take my game to places where I was challenged, and I just reached the point where I had gotten everything out of the college system in America. It felt like spending four years of juggling school and having to pass school to play golf, and screwing around with all the other kids in school, wasn't going to help me make it in golf.'

He becomes a card-carrying member of the European Tour. More beautiful than Apollo Belvedere, Zeus with a 5-iron, he attracts phone numbers from females at a rate last experienced by Alvin Purple. 'They're not groupies,' he protests. 'Just fans. I appreciate the fans.' He proves himself to be softly spoken, thoroughly decent and market-able until the end of time. More importantly, he can play. The first letter of invitation to the Masters arrives for the 2001 tournament.

'I don't really like to put any expectations on myself,' the 21-year-old says before his first look at the azaleas. 'If I'm smart out there, I'm sure I'll be around the pace. But I can't expect too much because there's so much local knowledge involved. I know it'll be nerve-racking: rolling in there for the first time, trying not to do anything stupid. Don't look like a rookie. But hopefully I can keep my composure and pull it off.'

If you believe in omens, you will enjoy this: Scott's first crack at Augusta National is a replica of the three-under 69 posted by Norman on debut. Problem being? None. Scott finishes tied for ninth with a couple of good old boys in Spain's Miguel Jimenez and a broad-shouldered, rambling bear of a man, El Pato, Argentina's Angel Cabrera.

Remember him.

··●··

Enter The Shark. 'Obviously when he was a young kid, everyone of Adam's vintage looked up to Greg,' says Phil Scott. 'We all watched when Greg was about to win the Masters every second bloody year, it seemed. And it never happened. As was the case for every Australian golf fan, Greg was it for us. He was the man. He led every major in '86 on the Saturday night. Virtually every time he teed it up, it

Bobby Jones (left, in 1932) is pictured in the early stages of transforming the 365-acre Fruitland Nurseries into Augusta National Golf Club. (Augusta National/Getty Images)

The familiar sting of defeat: Jim Ferrier is the first (and not the last) Australian runner-up when he finishes second to American Jimmy Demaret at the 1950 Masters. (Augusta National/Getty Images)

Bridesmaid: Bruce Crampton is trumped by the great Jack Nicklaus in 1972. (Gary Newkirk/Allsport)

Bridesmaid revisited: Peter Thomson wins five British Opens, but never a Masters. 'No regrets.' (Chris McGrath/Getty Images)

Ian Baker-Finch had three top-10 Masters' finishes to join the long list of Australians to have fallen short at Augusta. (David Cannon/Getty Images)

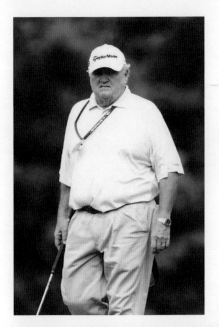

Charlie Epps, aka 'The Golf Doctor', is the most wholehearted and sincere supporter of Angel Cabrera. But he has no doubt that Adam Scott will drain his birdie putt on the second playoff hole to win the Masters, and his first major, in one fell swoop. 'I knew he was going to make it. It was destiny.' (Andrew Redington/Getty Images)

Craig Parry gives the Masters a shake in 1992 before being abused by intoxicated patrons rooting for American Fred Couples. 'Looking back on it, I should have handled it a little bit different.' (Timothy A. Clary/AFP/Getty Images)

Greg Norman loses the 1987 Masters when Augusta native Larry Mize chips in from next to the 11th green: 'That was destiny saying, You aren't going to win this tournament.' (Brian Morgan/Getty Images)

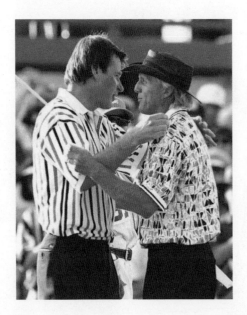

Norman bogeys the first. Five the difference. Faldo birdies the sixth. Four the difference . . . on it goes. Norman's tee shot on sixteen is pulled left. Splash. CBS's Peter Kostis tells 150 million television viewers: 'That's curtains.' Norman has relinquished a six-shot overnight lead to lose to Englishman Nick Faldo. 'Since '96, of everything that has transpired in my career, I am most proud of how I handled that loss.' (Doug Collier/AFP/ Getty Images)

Jack Newton goes toe-to-toe with Seve Ballesteros in 1980 before the Spaniard prevails. Cursed? 'That's a myth. There's no such thing.' (Peter Dazeley/Getty Images)

Facing page: Adam Scott leads the 2012 British Open by four strokes with four holes to play before a breakthrough major triumph slips through his fingers at Royal Lytham and St Annes. (Ross Kinnaird/Getty Images)

Left: Scott has just missed the putt that would have sent him into a playoff against Ernie Els at the 2012 British Open. (Glyn Kirk/AFP/Getty Images)

Els accepts the Claret Jug. He will travel by private jet to Augusta with Scott for a secret research-and-destroy mission before the 2013 Masters. (Peter Muhly/AFP/Getty Images)

Top left: Paradise found: South African Gary Player joins the legendary American duo of Jack Nicklaus and Arnold Palmer to perform the ceremonial tee-off on the morning of the first round at Augusta. (Andrew Redington/Getty Images)

Top right: Grand Master: Nicklaus is a six-time champion at Augusta. But he had to wait decades to receive his first green jacket. (Andrew Redington/Getty Images)

Left: Marc Leishman: 'Who knows, maybe we can take that Australian curse off.' (David Cannon/Getty Images)

looked like he would win whatever tournament he was in. I don't remember '86, but Adam would have been watching. And then '87, I certainly remember watching Larry Mize with Adam. That was a shattering experience for us.

'As Adam was getting better as a teenager and he started playing representative golf, and he started getting a little more exposed, he ran into Greg a couple of times through playing the big Australian tournaments as an amateur. He was heading to a tournament in Sydney and Greg got in touch to offer Adam a lift in his plane. For the life of me, I don't remember if he was going to play the Greg Norman International, or what it was. But I do remember the lift because we drove him to the airport. Greg had this schmick little whatever-it-was plane in those days. Sometimes now I think it was all a bit surreal. Adam was such a kid and Greg was a mega-star, a rock star, and Adam was jumping into his plane for a lift down to Sydney. Greg always kept in touch from there. None of it was especially big stuff, but he kept in touch to see how Adam was going.'

Examples?

'There was general discussion between us about the right time for Adam to turn pro and whether it should be in Europe or the States,' says Phil. 'Greg was really helpful with all that. I remember him speaking to Adam when we were in Vegas once, getting on the phone to him and having a good chat about Europe. Greg was really in favour of learning the craft a bit, which was the way Adam was heading anyway. I think between them in those early years, it was very much just a case of a young kid receiving advice from a seasoned pro. While none of us were privy to the exact conversations they had, it was just really solid advice that we appreciated.

'Maybe there's a perception of Greg that would give the wrong impression about the kind of input he would have. The way he normally talks about things, the way he is really definitive, it might make you think he says this is what you must do. That was never the impression I had at all. The impression was very much, "I'll tell you what I have learned and you make your own decisions." Whether it was his opinion on playing in Europe instead of America, telling Adam he couldn't say yes to everyone—just general things, a bit of advice from a bloke who had been around the block. So as much as the actual chats were important, the really important thing for Adam was the feeling that he could get on the phone to Greg whenever something was bothering him. It wasn't necessarily about what was said. It was more about Adam knowing he could ask Greg about anything at all. Even if it was something ridiculous.

'Greg had seen and done it all in golf, good and bad, as we know, which gave Adam the feeling that someone was in his corner who got it. Greg had seen the highest of highs and probably the biggest disappointments ever, so whatever Adam was going through, Greg had probably already been there. Then obviously as the years went on, Adam became less of a boy and more of a man, and their relationship changed. Adam would go and stay at Greg's place when he floated over to Florida. Now it was more man-to-man. The wily campaigner and the kid that might. It's nice, isn't it?'

Sure. Why did they click?

'Hindsight is dangerous territory,' says Phil. 'But number one, I think it's because Adam is non-offensive. Someone like Greg is almost the alpha-male, isn't he, and Adam wasn't a twenty-year-old who was in his face and questioning him constantly. Adam is a pretty respectful type of guy. He has stronger opinions than people probably realise, but I think because he's not a conflict sort of person, that probably helped. I would think Greg probably likes that around him: intelligence without conflict.

'And of course, the golf, looking at Adam and thinking jeez, this kid really could do it. Greg is no idiot. He can make a pretty good judgement call on a young fella's golf and I think when he saw Adam play, he probably thought he was worthy. Maybe that was the start. It must have been, because he didn't know Adam well enough to make a judgement on the person. He probably thought gosh, he's not an offensive kid, he has a bit of ability, I'm happy to spend some time here. I'm sure there have been periods when it hasn't been anything more than, "Let's have a beer." But as I said, the most tremendous and important part for Adam was knowing he had Greg's ear if he needed it.'

The most picturesque swing on the planet can be considered Phil's creation because he coached his son to the age of nineteen. He's travelled all the emotional and technical alleys with him and as such, whenever Adam receives the blessing of success, is Phil not miffed by the spotlight falling on the comparatively distant input of Norman?

'Not at all,' says Phil. 'I can't see why it would be

like that. I might have spent my whole life in golf and know a bit about it, but one thing I didn't do was play at the highest level. I could never assume to know what that would be like. Obviously, Greg knows all about it. I just always thought his advice was fantastic for Adam. We could give him two different things. Greg was able to offer Adam counsel and advice in an area that I was not qualified, i.e. playing golf at the highest level and understanding everything that went with it. My role was more about what anyone would do with their kids. It was just helpful that I understood golf and the golf business. Adam and I are good mates and with that, you take the good and the bad like all parents do with their kids. So Greg and I just had really different roles.

'A lot of people ask me if I feel like Greg gets all the credit and my answer is no. He receives credit for what he did because it was important. What he has done for Adam, he didn't have to do. He put his hand up and was happy to offer advice, and he didn't interfere. But we're both just components in it. I would equally pose the theory that neither of us is responsible for Adam's success.'

•• • ••

Scott wins titles of prestige in 2002: the Qatar Masters, the Scottish PGA. The victory margins are six and ten shots respectively. Comparisons with Woods are inevitable and constant. Initially flattered to be mentioned in the same breath as the apex predator, Scott grows tired of the perceived likenesses about, oh, five minutes after they begin. His bullet-train of a world ranking climbs to the clouds. Tournaments are won at Gleneagles in Scotland, Leopard Creek in South Africa, Pine Valley in China and the Stadium Course at TPC Sawgrass in Florida, the venue for the so-called fifth major, the Players Championship. Scott credits the most prestigious title of his burgeoning career to a chipping lesson and brainstorming session at Norman's palatial house in Florida.

When officialdom at the 2008 US Open at San Diego's Torrey Pines bowed to the promotions department and groups the top three players in the world for the prime-time television slot in the opening two rounds, Woods and Phil Mickelson are joined by the latest inductee to the highest echelon: Adam Derek Scott. His results in majors have been poor but aged 27 in a sport where peaks are mostly struck in the mid-30s, when sufficient emotional maturity has finally developed to combat the complexities of a strangely agonising solo endeavour, expectations of multiple major triumphs remain realistic and correctamundo. And so we wait. And wait. Scott finishes 26th at Torrey Pines while Woods wins his 14th major despite the inconvenience of a double stress fracture of his left tibia. For all intents, he has done it on one leg. Newton is commentating for Australian television and his frustrations with Scott are ready to explode.

'He was playing with Woods and Mickelson,' says Newton. 'You can't get much bigger than that. The US Open, the marquee group. They played the back nine first. He hit a great drive down 18. He had a 4-iron to the green and he hung it to the right. He had about a 40-footer. He hit the first putt twelve foot short and eight foot wide. I thought, "What was that?" Then he hit his putt up and it went past. Then he back-handed it and missed it. Then he holed it for a four-putt six. I thought, "Where is his head?" First of all, you wouldn't back-hand one at the US Open, playing with those two blokes, while the whole world was watching. I just thought it was weird stuff. I can't remember whether I said anything on TV about it, but when I eventually did ask him the question, he definitely wasn't going to like it. But what had I done wrong? I hadn't done anything to him.'

Scott has played with a broken hand. A friend smashed it in a car door the night of the Champions League football final in Russia. With an interlocking grip, Scott would have withdrawn. With his overlapping fingers, there was no discomfort. He has flown eight of his mates to San Diego and thrown them into a house near Torrey Pines, eating dinner with them every night and basking in the glow of his hoopla grouping. But he fizzles out of contention in his 29th major since his first at the 2000 British Open at St Andrews. The record is appalling in relation to the sugary promise: seven missed cuts and only one top-five finish from 29 starts. He limps home to the Gold Coast. We have a chat, up close and personal.

The venue is Sanctuary Cove's Cafe 19. Scott wears a suit. Jacket and tie have been removed on a humid day. He is open and honest. No subject is taboo, including matters of the broken heart. Twenty-three million dollars (and counting) in career prizemoney and another eight million a year in endorsements—and he's forgotten his wallet.

Too heavy to carry? Too large to fit in his pocket? Apologies for the pithiness. Scott orders a lemon, lime and bitters. He speaks of business: designing courses with Phil, his charity foundation. Why bother? Why not hoard your millions?

'The foundation was inspired by being in the States,' he says. 'Seeing the work the PGA Tour does, and just the attitude they have in the States to charity work, I really thought there was something I could do for my own community back here in Australia. As long as fifteen kids, or whatever the number might be, get to live a better lifestyle from us building the apartments we're putting down here, and they get the lifestyle they deserve, that's a nice thing to offer.' A seven-million-dollar complex on the Gold Coast is being constructed for the disadvantaged. 'It's funny how your outlook on money changes over time,' he says. 'At the start you have nothing and then it just accumulates. It depends what lifestyle you want to live. If I can give back something, I should. What I'm trying to say is, I'm pretty fortunate and I should be able to help people. I was surprised when I got to America and started on the tour and saw the attitude they all have to philanthropy. Being in that environment made me more aware of what can be done. For a lot of successful people and celebrities over there, it's a big thing to be involved in charities. Hopefully I can end up having an effect everywhere but right now, it's important to me that it's in my own community.

'The course design is something I enjoy doing with Dad. If I can make something half-decent, I'll have a go. Dad puts his two cents in, I put my two cents in. We eventually come up with something that looks good on paper, but I don't really have the passion to devote enough time to be full-on with it, and I don't see myself designing 40 courses around the world. I'd rather be putting time into the foundation and making sure that is established. It's a sensitive thing to be involved with. There are some touchy subjects and I want to make my charity legitimate, established and transparent so that it can be recognised for the work it's doing. I want Australia to feel like home to me still. We only have two events here a year and when you're away so much, it's bizarre that coming home feels like a holiday. I want to establish that presence back here in some way. We don't get to compete here enough for the public to see us. It's not like the cricketers, who have a tour over summer and are in the spotlight all the time.'

Scott speaks of surfing, of the energy source of the ocean, of catching waves in California and the Maldives and of how, in retirement, 'I see settling down one day as being at the beach and just falling out of bed into the surf every morning.' He speaks of Zen and the art of golf swing and lifestyle maintenance. 'I'd like to go to Everest,' he says. 'I'd like to climb to base camp. That's going to take a bit of doing because it's obviously quite time-consuming. I like the outdoors a lot. I've read the books and seen the videos about guys who have climbed Everest. I'd really like to look through Nepal and Bhutan. The whole area interests me, and I quite like the Buddhist philosophies. I just think they encourage well-being and the importance of being good people.'

He appears to be living it himself. 'Yeah, I'm pretty relaxed,' he says. 'I don't see any reason why I shouldn't be. Most things are pretty good. I tend not to sweat the small stuff.'

Where does the calm come from? 'It's not from my mum, that's for sure,' he laughs. 'I don't really know. I can't imagine being under stress and all that kind of stuff. For me, having what was a pretty tough break-up with my girlfriend—that was not a lot of fun and I don't want to live like that . . . we broke up earlier this year and it's been a pretty tough few months, actually. No doubt that had an effect on my performances towards the end of the year. It was tough because we were together for seven years. Even though we weren't married or anything like that, there was still a lot of stuff that had to be sorted out. I certainly wasn't planning on it but I guess you learn a lot from those kinds of situations. It definitely had an effect on my golf because my head was elsewhere, my practice was down.

'It was a tough time, but that's life. It's been nice to get back into relaxed mode, but it's taken a few months. Definitely taken a while. We were taking a break and then we decided to call it quits. After seven years—that's a long time. It took me a while to get my head around it all. My life changed a lot. We lived together in London for five years and had built a home here because she was going to move down here. Going back to our place in London, it's not ideal. It's a nice house. But things change.'

He speaks of health issues. 'I've been battling some infection that keeps coming back,' he says.

'That's really interrupted everything, too. There was a period where I didn't practise for so long. To be honest, I think it was a bit of a fatigue thing. Every time I got run down, it came on. It was a year of a lot of crap going on.'

He has seen nothing yet. He speaks of Phil: 'There have been times when it's been really difficult. He travelled with me a fair bit, early days. As you grow up, there are points where he's known to step away. And there have been times when I have had to step away a little bit. That's all tough stuff. At the start of my career, it was fantastic having him there. He's handled everything really well. I'm sure some of it has been tough for him to swallow. Some of it has been tough for me to swallow. But that's what life is all about, I guess. He's been in golf all his life and no doubt he wanted to see me give it a shot when he saw I had potential.'

He speaks of his failures at majors. Do you have the courage to win one? You know there are doubters. 'I don't pay much attention to what is written about my golf or said about my golf,' he says. 'It's all got to come from within anyway. If my career goes by and I don't win one, then maybe I'll have to question my own desire. The way I look at it, so what if I win one major? I will be a bloke forgotten anyway. If I've won one major, am I going to be satisfied with that? No. I'm not looking to win one major. I'd like to win more than one. Winning one major—I'll be asked so, was it a fluke that you won one? Is that what I'll get asked ten years after I win it? I don't think winning one justifies anything. I would like to win a lot of majors. I can win five tournaments a year for the rest of my career but I know if I don't win a major, I will probably feel incomplete. I need to focus on winning a major. I would rather get it out of the way at the Masters in April and not get asked it again. Ask me again in five years.'

Shall do.

•• • ••

Enter the Coach. His following year is horrible. Scott misses the cut at the Masters. And the Open. Addressing the ball in 2009, he develops only a vague idea about where it might go. The freefall is uncomfortable to the point of being unwatchable. He ties for 36th at the US Open after a brief session with a different mentor, his brother-in-law, Brad Malone. Food for thought. His world ranking plummets from three to 63. He is 108th on the US Tour's money list. He risks losing his card and being forced back to a minor tour with all the dunderheads taking their canyons for divots. Armchair critics are in abundance. He is too soft. A show pony. Lacking in commitment. He is the worst putter in the history of humankind.

Scott misses six consecutive cuts in the States—six straight weekends without golf. The equivalent to golfing unemployment. 'A terrible feeling,' he says. Every week provides a fresh opportunity, however, and Minnesota's Hazeltine course is the venue for the final major of the year, the PGA Championship. Scott opens with a humiliating 82. He follows it with a 79. He misses the cut and nearly finishes last. Something has to give, and his name is Butch Harmon. Enter the brother-in-law.

Englishman Brad Malone is a decent player with a serviceable rather than a lightning-bolt swing. He is hedging his career bets by dabbling in a coaching traineeship in case he doesn't make the grade as a player. Malone is a mate of England player Justin Rose, who has befriended Scott on the European PGA Tour. Scott's sister, Casie, is moving to London to study physiotherapy, and Scott asks

Rose to help her settle in. 'Adam told Justin if you're having any dinner parties or whatever, invite Casie over because it would be nice for her to meet a few friends,' says Malone. 'I met Casie then.'

One of the perks of dating Casie Scott is jagging eighteen holes with Adam at the Queenwood Golf Club in west London, an exclusive setting with Augusta-esque privacy and Hugh Grant counted among its membership. Scott shows Malone his future in the shape of one searing 4-iron to bullet the grey sky.

'It was all the confirmation I needed that there was no longer a need for me to play,' says Malone. 'Because I knew I could stand there all day long and never be as good as that. There was this one shot. I remember standing behind Ad on this par three. It was a windy, overcast day, and we were straight into the wind. It must have been about 230 yards. Adam hit a 4-iron and he just flushed it, straight through the wind and straight at the pin. It just tore off the club face, and that was it for me. I told myself, I can't ever do that. It really was quite intimidating. I must have been off a handicap of about two at the time, so I could get it around. But it was a turning point because that was just a whole different level of striking a golf ball. It's a different noise, a different ball flight. The power and speed and quality was phenomenal. To that point, I certainly enjoyed playing and working on my own game, but I realised then that you needed that extra level of talent to really excel. It put the nail in the coffin for me as a player.'

Malone throws himself into his traineeship at Surrey's Wentworth club. Inquisitive genes have triggered an eagerness to understand the mechanics of the golf swing. 'Dad was an engineer and he likes the inner workings of things, tinkering and finding out how things work and problem solving,' says Malone. 'That got me into trying to understand how I could improve my own game. Why is the ball not flying where I want it to fly? The answer is in developing a correct and repetitive ball flight. Everybody's swing is different. How we move as individuals is unique. But if you can do something that repeats and is correct, producing a very similar outcome time after time, you're never going to go too far wrong.'

Malone returns to Australia, with Casie, to be the professional at the Arundel Hills Golf Club on the Gold Coast. He's a disciple of John Jacobs, the

English coach, writer and Hall of Fame resident who wrote one of the best-received golf books in existence, *Golf Doctor*. 'John Jacobs wrote the book on coaching,' says Butch Harmon. 'There is not a teacher out here who doesn't owe him something.'

Malone is among them. 'I don't teach one golf swing,' he says. 'My philosophy is that the fix is very unique to the individual. Any advice I give, from the amateur to the tour professional, is to simply make the ball flight more consistent. Take a guy who comes to our club hitting a slice. As long as he goes home not hitting a slice, he goes home happy. Rather than giving him a pretty back swing that still slices, I'd rather give him something that cures the thing stopping him from enjoying his golf. And that's the path of his ball. For Adam, at the very top level, it was about the height of his shots and the spin rate.'

Scott has one request. He wants the steepling trajectory and commanding backspin required to win the Masters.

'Things had run their course with Butch,' says Phil. 'He's a great guy, and he did a lot of great stuff with Ad, but sometimes these things have a shelf life. It's not always the player. It can be at either end. Your focus goes somewhere else. The intensity is gone and it all seems a bit boring. Brad had done some work with Adam leading into the US Open that year—he was playing really poorly before then, but he played quite well after working with Brad. Nothing much happened for a while because it had only been a stop-gap. It took another few months for Adam and Butch to accept the fact their time was done. There wasn't serious fall-out or anything nasty at all, but it just took a bit of time for the reality to hit home that hey, listen, we're done.'

Explains Scott: 'I think it was just a matter of bad habits creeping in over time. They were really hard for me to get rid of while playing at the same time. I wish I'd taken a month off earlier in the year and just gone to the range and grinded it out and not come back until I was on top of it. To do it while continuing to play, that was tough.'

'He just said to me, I want a second opinion,' says Malone. 'I think a few of his fundamentals had slipped too far. Adam is obviously very naturally talented, his ability is immense, but a few of the basics had fallen away and affected his swing in a way that made him too reliant on timing on a day-to-day basis. When your swing becomes timing-reliant, and you lose a bit of confidence, that's when you're going to get into trouble.

'For any golfer, when you're hitting it both ways, when you're missing shots to the right and the left, it's a confidence knocker because you don't know where to aim. You end up aiming straight and hoping for the best. What you need to do is eliminate one side of the course. So even if your rhythm is out, or you're mis-hitting the ball, you know it's either going to go straight or in Adam's case, slightly to the right. He needed to eliminate the other side of the course. And then we needed to evaluate why, having obviously won a lot of golf tournaments to that point, and being one of the very top players out there, third in the world, why was this guy not contending in majors when he was winning PGA tournaments?

'Even before that 2009 season, when things obviously didn't pan out like Ad wanted, he hadn't contended in the majors as often as he wanted to, or as often as people thought he should. He really felt, and I agreed with him, that the ball flight was too low to hold on the greens at the big tournaments. That was part of the whole process of putting together a game that was able to compete.

We needed a universal ball flight that he could use at an Open championship in the wind, or on those greens at the Masters.'

They have begun their climb to Augusta National.

••●••

Scott is at his lowest ebb after Hazeltine. Re-enter Norman as captain of the International team for the Presidents Cup clash against the United States in San Francisco. Norman can field his ten highest-ranked players, plus two of his own choosing. He can pluck Billy Dunk out of retirement if he so desires. Norman's first choice is Japan's Ryo Ishikawa. Scott's train wreck of a year should leave him a country mile out of the equation but Norman throws the dog a bone.

Howls of protest. In *Golf Digest*: 'As a Presidents Cup contestant, he [Scott] is now eligible to automatically compete in many events he would otherwise not be eligible for. In essence, he has a free PGA Tour ride for two years. Greg Norman is shamelessly trying to save Scott's career at the expense of his dignity and duty to his team. There were similar charges levelled at Gary Player when he chose Trevor Immelman back in 2005. Why is Norman not getting the criticism he deserves?'

Is he ever! From *Golf World*: 'Then pick number two goes to fellow Aussie Adam Scott and I thought, now he's really gone mad. The more you look at it, the more insane it becomes. Scott is currently in a funk of possibly catastrophic proportions. Take a look at his results in his last thirteen events where there was a halfway cut to be made: Cut, cut, cut, cut, cut, cut, T64, cut, T36, cut, cut, cut, T58. Does that, in any way, resemble the record of any other captain's pick in the entire history of captain's picks? Only Norman would take such a gamble when logic would dictate otherwise. It's almost as if he is trying to spark Scott into resuming his form of over a year ago. He said the pick of Scott was "a no-brainer". That phrase would more likely be applied to himself.'

ESPN's analyst Dottie Pepper turns a blind eye to the real dimensions of human tragedy by telling Scott he is sinking faster than the *Titanic*. 'As for the second pick, Adam Scott, all I can say is: Wow!' she writes. 'His world ranking has sunk from No. 3; he's missed the cut in ten of his eighteen starts on tour this year; and his health is a concern. Scott is a tremendous guy to be around and possesses a scary amount of talent, but the Presidents Cup has two alternate-shot sessions, and he must play in at least one of them. How do you put a guy who's 159th in driving accuracy, 165th in greens in regulation and 189th in putting in that situation?'

The disbelief is just as evident in Australia. The respected and experienced Martin Blake writes in *The Age* newspaper in Melbourne: 'But in selecting Scott to play in the Presidents Cup in San Francisco next month as his captain's pick, Norman has made an error. Scott does not need this right now, at the end of his worst season on the American tour, a time when he is wrestling with his game as any young professional will do at some stage. There will be too much pressure on Scott to perform and as an extension of this, Norman's credibility as captain of the International team also goes on the line.'

We remind Norman of the kerfuffle. 'When you have belief in someone's game, ability and character, you have to shut out what everyone else might be saying and just go with your heart,' he says. 'You either trust your instincts, or you don't. I've always tried to trust mine. People get down in a funk for certain reasons and it may not always be their game. There might be other reasons in their life. Sometimes just a little vote of confidence from somebody allows you to think differently and approach life differently.' But Scott was awful at the time. 'I picked Adam because I thought he was going to be a great asset to the team,' says Norman. 'That was the bottom line. Not only from a play-ability standpoint, but from the standpoint of him being a valuable team member. He's a very popular guy. It wasn't going to be difficult to find someone to play with him.'

And yet it is. Scott is still a horror show when he arrives in San Fran. Another missed cut at the Wyndham Championship. A tie for 58th at the Barclays. Thirty-fifth at the Turning Stone Championship, where the spin on his irons is so savage that his ball keeps hitting greens and sucking clean off them. He flies from JFK Airport on the Sunday night.

'It was very up in the air which way Greg would go,' he says. 'It was quite flattering to be picked and to play under Greg is a great honour. I've been working my arse off for three weeks trying to get my game as good as I possibly can. I don't need a kick in the pants to work hard. I've never worked harder in my life than this year.'

Scott's complaisant nature is sparking murmurs about lost motivation. That he couldn't care less about his career. 'It's disappointing when people get that impression,' he says. 'I've hit so many golf balls and worked so hard. That's been the frustrating part, to get no results from all the hard work. Some of it, I think it will be just about getting my set-up straightened out. That feels better straight away and then it will just be a matter of finding a bit of confidence.'

He is cramming for an exam he is ill-prepared for. 'It had been a long, hard year and he was struggling, obviously,' says Malone. 'When he found out about the Presidents Cup, we met up the week before and started working on it. Things hadn't been going as he wanted. Initially, on a technical level, it was about how strong his left-hand grip had become. From there, the knock-on was that his alignment was quite a long way to the left. From there, the ball position would get too far back in his stance. Which meant the swing had developed quite an in-to-out path. When that happens, for Adam especially, it's not going to hold up for four days because all he has left is the timing.

'So we started by addressing the most fundamental thing of all, the grip. It was all with a long-term view in mind because he had made one thing very clear to me. He told me, "Major championships are what I'm after". The ball flight had to be high because traditionally at majors, the greens are hard and fast. Your approaches have to be spinning and landing softly. A lot of the swing changes made were for consistency, but we were also keeping the question in mind, how will this affect the ball flight? Is it going to make it better for majors? We had to find that balance. It was quite a process but Adam really embraced it.

'Being picked for the Presidents Cup team was definitely a big confidence booster, but he had to complement that by making sure he was doing the right things technically. It's amazing with a player of Adam's calibre, when he knows he can make certain movements with confidence and he knows he has the ball under control, how quickly he can get his game back.'

·· ● ··

Enter Cabrera. Professional golfers are an eccentric and superstitious bunch and while Scott is universally respected and warmly greeted in San Francisco, most of his teammates run for the hills when it comes time to raise their hands and volunteer to partner him. They fear his afflicted game may be contagious. Ernie Els and Angel Cabrera are the exceptions. Els, the South African with a swing laid-back enough to be snoring at the moment of impact. Cabrera, the Argentinian sensitive to struggle because he has endured a lifetime of it: raised by his grandmother from the age of two after his parents gave him up when they divorced; leaving school as a ten-year-old to work as a caddie in Cordoba and put food on his grandmother's table; arriving barefoot for his first day on a bag because he was unable to afford shoes.

Cabrera did what all caddies do in their downtime, belting balls on the range, and his homegrown swing became a rocket launcher. Aged twenty, he was encouraged by Argentina's tour player Eduardo Romero to try his luck as a player. Cabrera failed on three straight occasions to earn his European PGA card. Romero financed a fourth and last attempt, and Cabrera snuck through. He won the 2009 US Masters to complete his rags-to-majors tale and earn himself a gig at the Presidents Cup.

Scott's first partner at the Presidents Cup is Els. 'I haven't worked with Butch for a couple of months,' he announces before their two-and-one defeat of Hunter Mahan and Sean O'Hair. A win! Norman is looking less the ignoramus already. 'I've always had a good feeling about Adam,' says Els. 'He's had a bit of a tough season, but talent never goes. There's always pressure on the captain's pick to justify their place, so what Adam went through today was very difficult. Before the first tee shot, I could see he was quite riled up, and he nailed it about 350 down the fairway. He played awesome golf.'

Scott is beaming. 'You get pumped up, it takes a while to calm down,' he says. 'My first chip was pretty average, a nervy one. After a couple of holes, I got into the flow of it. Any victory for the team is important but for me personally, obviously it feels great.'

Then it goes pear-shaped. Playing with another South African, Retief Goosen, in the Friday morning four-ball, Scott loses three-and-two to Justin Leonard and Phil Mickelson. Back with The Big Easy, Els, in the Saturday morning foursomes, he succumbs four-and-two to Leonard and Jim Furyk. The swings of Scott and Furyk: compare and contrast. Eye-candy versus effectiveness. The latter is preferable. In the Saturday afternoon four-ball, the chain-smoking Cabrera shoulders Scott's substantial load in a two-down loss to Furyk and Anthony Kim. Furyk! Scott slumps to a four-and-three defeat to Stewart Cink in the Sunday singles.

'In truth, I don't think Adam played particularly well at the Presidents Cup,' concedes Phil Scott. 'But it was important because it was the start of him regaining some confidence. He was in the middle of a slump but I think being selected by Greg said to Adam, "They haven't lost faith in me".'

'So disappointing,' says Scott. 'It was a tough week. I played okay, but not good enough. That's the way it goes but it was a big moment for me. It was kind of gut-check time. My game was in a bit of a rut and I wasn't enjoying it so much, but Greg had a lot of faith in me. He gave me a pick and I didn't want to disappoint him. Thinking back on it, what that did was automatically put me into a situation of playing world-class golf again. There's no hiding in a Presidents Cup. You have to go out against the best players in the world, and I used that as a real motivator to remember I could be a great player again. If you don't have that opportunity to be in that environment, sometimes it's very hard to play yourself out of a rut in a tournament. But I was put in that situation of playing under pressure again, and I needed that. I took the ball from there and ran with it. It was a big boost for me.'

More than the validation derived from Norman's unbending support, Scott is revved up by six words from Cabrera.

'Angel is a great man,' says Scott. 'I've played with him a couple of times in Presidents Cup, spent some time with him—he said a great thing to me. He pulled me aside and he said, "You are a great, great player." It was something I wouldn't forget.'

·· ● ··

Enter Momentum. Next stop, Singapore. The Australian Masters and Australian Open are on the horizon. Scott is yet to have his name deep-etched on either of the most prestigious trophies in his homeland. More aberrations. His warm-up will be at the Singapore Open. When he limps out of the Presidents Cup, the parallels with Ian Baker-Finch's terminal decline have become alarming. The similarities in personalities and career free-falls.

Baker-Finch has won the 1991 Open Championship at Royal Birkdale by ripping through the front nine on the Sunday in 29 shots. Then swing changes sent him into the abyss. If it ain't broke—he tried to fix it anyway. At Royal Troon in 1997, he shoots a gut-churning 92, twenty-one over par, in a scene so grizzled that it sickens the most hardened of British sports writers. Reports Ian Wooldridge in *The Daily Mail*: 'In a world disfigured by famine and violence, one must be cautious about using the word "tragic" in the context of sporting misfortune. But, by God, it was a close run thing at the Open Championship yesterday. For what befell Ian Baker-Finch in four-and-a-half hours over the dunes of the Ayrshire coast was far more than misfortune. It was like watching a great surgeon whose hands have started to tremble or a concert pianist who has utterly lost his nerve. In the end, spectating became sheer voyeurism, intrusion into private grief. It shouldn't have happened to a dog, let alone a charming 36-year-old Australian who, just six years ago, won the Open title at Royal Birkdale. Yesterday, Baker-Finch simply couldn't play golf.'

Drives disappear into 18 inches of gorse. Irons land on moonscape territory. 'In similar conditions—windy, but never ultimately testing by Royal

Troon's uncompromising standards—complete golfing illiterates have bettered his 21-over-par 92,' writes Wooldridge. 'It was not a fall from grace because, throughout, his grace never left him. Many would have feigned injury and withdrawn to spare themselves further embarrassment.

'But Baker-Finch battled onwards. Escaping under false pretences was beneath his dignity. Indeed, at the 12th, he looked up at the 30 or so of us at the scene of his misfortune, spread his hands in helplessness and actually laughed. In fact, he played a miraculous recovery shot but he never laughed thereafter. It says everything for the generosity of golf galleries that everyone was willing him on. But it was beyond him and the last act was inevitable. This most genial and cooperative of sportsmen walked blank-eyed past reporters, slipped an arm around his wife, left the premises and later formally announced he had withdrawn. I doubt whether we shall ever see him play championship golf again.'

Baker-Finch has received advice from all manner of crackpots. 'Weird stuff, like people sent me rocks,' he tells *Golf Digest*. '"Sleep for six weeks with this rock under the left side of your pillow, and then put it under the right side of the pillow and keep it in your left pocket at all times. This has worked for me. This is my gift.'" He is offered the use of a mud spa in Italy that will exorcise the swing demons. The offer is politely rejected.

'It's amazing how quickly it slides when you lose your confidence,' he says. 'I was in the top 25 in the world from 1986 to 1992. When you start falling . . . at the end of '92, I was 24th in the world and I thought the world had come to an end. I thought, holy shit, how can I be 24 in the world? But by the end of '93, I was out of the fifties. By the end of '94, I was probably barely in the 200s. Adam was a top-ten player, and he should never have been outside of that top ten, so that was a really big slide he was going through. I was confident he would find his way back, although maybe not to the same level he was before. Sometimes guys go through a hard time and they find it difficult to recover, but sometimes you're only one great shot away from your next great round, your next great tournament and your next jump back up the ladder. We're all pretty fragile when it comes to dealing with issues. Unfortunately for me, I worked on it the wrong way. I worked on it as hard as I could but I did it the wrong way. I know that now.'

The silver lining to Baker-Finch's plight is that it has expedited his career as an analyst of the highest calibre for CBS in America. He has been a constant presence at Scott's tournaments, but never have they discussed Baker-Finch's grey period while Scott is experiencing his own.

'I didn't go there with Adam,' says Baker-Finch. 'I was just always there for him as a sounding board. I don't want it to sound like he came up to the commentary booth and dragged me out on the putting green, but I was always there and if I saw him, I'd go over and say g'day. I just wanted him to know he had a friend if he needed one. I know his family well, we still catch up for a coffee at Sanctuary Cove when I go home.

'I've known him since he was a young teenager and have been following him for twenty years, so there's a natural interest in him. I haven't been the mentor that Greg has been, but I've tried to help. They all grew up idolising Greg and he was No. 1 in the world. Having Greg putting him in the Presidents Cup was a huge moment in Adam's career, at just the right time. I think afterwards, there was that little bit more determination because of Greg's faith in him. It was a big move, and Adam can always thank Greg for that because until then, it was like Adam was falling off the face of the earth.'

•• ● ••

Enter the Recovery. No need for sleeping for six weeks with a rock under the left side of his pillow. The surgeon's hands are about to stop trembling. Scott begins his Singapore swing with a pair of 72s. And then it clicks. A 65 in the third round at Sentosa Golf Club is the flicking of the switch. Malone's meddling has done the trick.

'What Ads went through in that 2009 period, he had never felt like that before in his life,' says Malone. 'And he's never felt like it again. I said one thing to him that always stands true with players like him: you never lose your talent, you only lose your form. It's about identifying why the form was lost. He made a huge change to his grip before that tournament and it felt really uncomfortable, but it enabled him to take out one whole side of the golf course. Weakening his grip was the start of solving the puzzle, and Singapore is where the penny dropped. I think that's where the confidence started to return. Certainly for me, I saw an instant change. Right before he went to Singapore, I remember thinking, "Gee, this is looking good on the range". He was really swinging the club freely, and I had a very strong sense that the technique was going to hold up from there.

'He sent me a text message from Singapore on the Thursday or Friday that said: "I really have a feeling for this now". He was hitting it as good as ever.' It's on the Saturday when Scott produces the number to match the mood. A closing 68 leaves him in a tie for third. *Sometimes you're only one great shot away from your next great round, your next great tournament and your next jump back up the ladder.* One of the questions at his press conference at Sentosa begins: 'You've had a horrible year, Adam . . .' He smiles in the belief the dog days are over. He has an unexpected spring in his step when he arrives at Melbourne's statuesque Kingston Heath for the Australian Masters. Tiger Woods is waiting, and so is Jack Newton. The half-baked four-putt at Hazeltine is still stuck in his craw.

When Scott takes his leather seat for his pre-Masters press conference, Newton grabs a chair behind the scribes. Now, these formal interviews before tournaments are normally genteel affairs. The majority of reporters are full-time football writers up to their necks in scandal all winter. They fancy a relaxed couple of weeks at the golf in summer. Questions from the floor are along the lines of, How are you hitting 'em, mate? So and so still your coach? Why? Why not? Like the course? Hate the course? Cheers for your time. Scott's interviews can stray towards the bland but he's well-liked by the scribblers. His year has been nothing short of a catastrophic mess on the whole, but he will be spared a grilling. Routine inquiries are lodged before Newton loses patience and cuts to the chase. Why does your putting suck? Words to the effect. Scott takes exception. Their relationship will be strained for years.

'I don't sit in the commentary box and criticise people because I want to criticise them,' says Newton. 'I try to offer, at all times, constructive criticism. As I went on to say, the problem was that he was such a good ball striker that he gave himself a lot of chances. Any golfer knows that if you keep missing chances, it does your head in. He needed to change something because he was wasting so many shots. I thought, does he need glasses or something? Because he didn't appear to be even reading the putts right. A lot of times it wasn't that he put a bad stroke on them. It seemed that he didn't know how to read them. It does your head in because when you get back to playing in the States, the Yanks are all putting the eyes out of it. Our Australian guys are technically a lot better than most of the Americans, but they don't have the same short game. I think Adam was in denial.'

Scott finishes sixth as Woods wins the gold jacket in the tournament that triggers revelations of his extra-marital affairs. All 121 of them, as he admits. 'It's quite interesting, really, because I remember Ads playing at Kingston Heath when Tiger won, and he just played unbelievable golf,' says Malone. 'Tee to green, it was just impeccable. As good as I think I have ever seen. It was amazing ball-striking but his putting was still off. There had been a lot of emphasis on fixing the long game and getting that to a point where he was comfortable, but the putting wasn't where he wanted or needed it to be.'

To the United Arab Emirates for the Dubai World Championships. 'Funny course,' says Scott. 'You just kind of plod your way around between the bunkers.' Seventh. Flying! He whistles through the front gates of the ocean-exposed, wind-whipped

New South Wales course at Sydney's La Perouse for the Australian Open.

The 113th edition of the national championship becomes organised chaos: gale-force winds force a five-hour postponement. Balls are blown off the greens. Fans, players, caddies, John Daly and every last one of us feel likely to be blown into the Pacific Ocean. On day three, the intoxicating sniff of contention back in his nostrils, the electricity back in his fingertips, Scott birdies 17 and 18 to lead Stuart Appleby by two.

'It's there for me with a good round tomorrow,' he says. 'For an Aussie, in a sense, this is like the next major. It would be something to savour.' Scott dines with Norman on the Saturday night. He wins the tournament in a canter. He pumps his fists after a four-shot triumph that ensures another invitation to Augusta. Rollicking momentum off the back of the Presidents Cup has catapulted him back inside the top 50 in the world. The beauty of golf, and sport: if you perform, you will be suitably rewarded. 'It's so bizarre, this game,' he says. 'Coming from such a bad year, to play well enough to win down here, I mean, it's just a crazy game.'

He joins luminaries such as Nicklaus, Palmer,

Watson, Player and Norman on the Stonehaven Cup. 'I kept thinking it would happen, but sometimes it just doesn't,' he says. 'The best athletes in the world go out and get it. They're not that patient, they make it happen and that's why they're the best. I had to look down this year and be really honest with myself and say: "How much do you want this?" I am so proud to be the champion of my own country. It's the pinnacle, really. I'm just thinking about the names on this trophy and I'm just so happy to be on there. It's something I'll treasure forever.'

He crosses paths with Norman between the 18th green and the scorer's hut. 'He's got to be feeling very good about himself,' says Norman. There's a man-hug. An exchange of pleasantries. Did Norman just kiss him on the cheek?! 'We're not that close,' grins Scott. 'He just said, "It's about bloody time."' When the moment comes beneath New South Wales' regal and jam-packed clubhouse for Scott to receive the 117-year-old silverware, the honour is performed by Norman. They trade banter and exchange roles. Scott has become what Norman used to be. The hope.

3

BRITISH OPEN AND SHUT

'I felt like knee-capping him.'
Phil Scott

Jack Newton is right. The putting is still out of whack. Scott's drives have the hang time of Air Force One and the irons are soaring at umpteen revolutions per minute but the short stick remains cross-eyed and misbehaving. Baker-Finch becomes something of a blade whisperer. 'Quite often at tournaments through 2010, I'd spend time with Adam on the putting green, just giving my thoughts on how to simplify it all,' he says. The putting, the putting, the putting. Scott's screaming ambition to win majors will never be realised without the putting. Even in dire moments, Baker-Finch could negotiate greens with neither spot nor wrinkle.

'It's not like Adam had a bad stroke,' he says. 'He did everything the right way and was trying to make himself better. He was just dealing with not performing at the level he wanted to. He wouldn't have gone as far as he did if he couldn't putt at all. I always thought he tried to be too perfect with the short putter, and he became too wooden. He didn't look natural and relaxed like he did with his long game.'

Scott compiles a serviceable 2010: a win at the Texas Open; top tens at the WGC Bridgestone Invitational, the Barclays and the Deutsche Championships; US$2.4 in prizemoney. But the code is yet to be cracked at the majors, so it is yet to be cracked at all. He ties for 18th at the Masters. Misses the cut at the US Open. Ties for 27th at the British Open. Ties for 39th at the PGA Championship. Run-of-the-mill. Making up the numbers. His ball-striking is all majors. His putting is the old Hooters Tour. Scott is busy missing the cut at the Sony Open in Hawaii at the beginning of 2011 when Malone wanders through the sliding doors of a Drummonds golf shop in the Gold Coast suburb of Ashmore.

'They had this putter that caught my eye,' he says. 'A long putter. I took it home and had a putt with it. There were a lot of things it promoted in my putting stroke that I thought would benefit Adam. It wasn't like he was hitting putts willy-nilly with a short putter. He wasn't that bad, but he didn't seem to be making much progress. A key problem was how hard he was trying. He lost being relaxed enough to let the putter swing naturally and freely. It's when you start over-analysing and over-thinking that it disrupts your natural thinking.'

The broomstick carries a stigma. Is this not an admission of defeat? Are the anchored putters not the domain of old men and grandmothers with the yips? 'I suggested to him, "You know, Ads, you should have a go with this,"' says Malone. 'He's a smart guy. There wasn't major reservation. He picked it up, had a go and after a bit of time of using it, he thought, "I like the feeling I'm getting here."'

Scott returns to America with a Scotty Cameron design from Titleist. 'The long putter was a completely new skill that he had never done before in his life,' says Malone. 'That was what he needed. There were no bad habits because he didn't have any habits. He was starting his putting from scratch.

He's a great athlete and it freed him from his old thoughts. He could go back to using the side of his brain which is just about instinct. Natural ability became the main component again, and that's when Adam was going to make progress.'

The impact is immediate. Scott ties for sixth at the WGC Bridgestone Invitational. Ties for fourth at the Tavistock Cup. Ties for second at the Masters. He's the clubhouse leader with another Australian, Jason Day, in a grandstand finish: eight players share the lead on the Sunday. Scott has romped home with a 67. Day lands a monster birdie putt on 17, and then another on 18. What a thing! Emphasising the truly global nature of the centuries-old sport, a representative of every continent on earth except Antarctica is given a taste of the lead.

At one stage on the back nine, there's a five-way tie for first. Irishman Rory McIlroy has held a four-shot overnight lead before labouring to an 80, losing by ten. Greg Norman can eat his heart out. Scott and Day are set for an all-Australian playoff for sheep stations but Charl Schwartzel, a mostly unthreatening South African quietly desperate to follow in the footsteps of Gary Player, birdies the last four holes to win by two. Never before has there been such a blazing finish. Most likely, never again. Another gross disappointment for Australian golf. Another hex on the nation. The closest shave for Scott.

'In 2011 we started working with the long putter, the putting improves, and that's when you see the ball-striking and putting collide, and that's when we start to see some good results in the majors,' says Malone. 'A second place at the Masters, I think he finished seventh at the PGA. The US Open that year he missed the cut but if you start to look through the major championships from there, the amount of top tens are starting to add up.'

··●··

The broomstick looks wrong. 'I'm okay with anyone saying that,' says Scott. 'And I'm okay with anyone who says it should not have been allowed in the first place. I mean, I could be one of the guys who would say that. But that's not the position we have. It has been there a long time and it is established in the game. They say now they want to change it because it's to the detriment of the game—show me the evidence it's hurting the game. There is none. Neither is there any evidence it gives an advantage, and there is no evidence that more people are using it. They say it is not a proper stroke but previous committees reviewed it and found nothing wrong. So this is a subjective view and subject to the whims of the committee of the day and I can't get my head around that.' But you have a vested interest. Clearly. You use one.

Norman wants it banned. Tiger Woods wants it banned. Norman's argument is that professional golfers should have enough skill and nerve to putt in the traditional manner. He expects it to be outlawed and he will be proved right just months after the Masters. 'I think the decision is going to be made; I think it has already been made,' says Norman. 'I think it's good for the game of golf that the R&A and the USGA are going to collaborate on this. It's the right thing. I think that professional golfers who have the technique and physical strength to extract maximum performances out of their technology, I think there should be restrictions put on that. I think the USGA and R&A will implement the ban and when the rule comes into effect, I think the broomstick will disappear.'

'Never been a fan,' says Woods. 'My idea is to have the rules so that the putter will be equal to or less than the shortest club in your bag. And I think with that, we'd be able to get away from any type of belly anchoring. I believe putting is the art of controlling the body and club and swinging the pendulum motion. That's how it should be played. I'm a traditionalist when it comes to that.'

'I won seventeen tournaments with the short putter,' says Scott. 'Two with the long putter. I just don't believe it is fair to say to professional players, "This is a legal putter," and some professionals go away and spend thousands of hours learning the skill of using the long putter . . . they spend two or three years of their careers getting this right, then the authorities say, "We're now going to make it illegal". To me, that is what's wrong.'

●●●●●

Blurred lines. One cup or two?

Caddies lend themselves to nicknames: Iron Man, Thirsty, Squeaky, Jelly, Tip, Golf Ball, Last Call, First Call, Due North, Eight Count, Gypsy, The Judge, The Growler, The Punk, Killer, Irish, Wheelbarrow, Ant Man, Bullet, Biggie, Chick, Munster, Skillet, Pepsi and Bones. New Zealand's Steve Williams could have a thousand monikers.

But he has none. He's just Stevie. Steve-ee! He had a handicap of two when he was thirteen, but quit playing to be a caddy. It's always been rumoured that as a sixteen-year-old he lied about his age so Norman would hire him. They were together for seven years before a combustible finish. Legend says that during a fight on their last day, Williams threw his soon-to-be-former boss in a swimming pool.

Also the looper for Raymond Floyd in his early days, the New Zealander is snapped up by Tiger Woods when Mike 'Fluff' Cowan is given the flick after the Nissan Open at Riviera in 1999. His thirteen-year association with Woods produces phenomenal success: 72 titles worldwide and thirteen majors.

Williams is unaware Woods has withdrawn from the US Open until after he arrives in the States from New Zealand. He works with Adam Scott instead, and the Australian misses the cut. Two weeks later, Woods waits until Scott has finished his final round of the AT&T at Pennsylvania's Aronimink course before taking Williams to a private room. His services are no longer required. The British Open is only a fortnight away. The split is to be kept quiet from the media out of respect to Scott. Initially, a circus will be avoided.

The player claims the split is amicable. The caddie disagrees. 'I want to express my deepest gratitude to Stevie for all his help, but I think it's time for a change,' Woods writes on his website. 'Stevie is an outstanding caddie and a friend and has been instrumental in many of my accomplishments. I wish him great success in the future.'

Williams is in his American summer home in Oregon when it becomes official. True to the modern mode of communication, he posts on his website: 'I am no longer caddying for Tiger after he informed me that he needed to make a change. After thirteen years of loyal service, needless to say this came as a shock. Given the circumstances of the past eighteen months, working through Tiger's scandal, a new coach and with it a major swing change, and Tiger battling through injuries, I am very disappointed to end our successful partnership.'

'A player has the right to fire a caddie at any given time,' says Williams. 'When a player is not playing at his best for an extended period of time, it's not uncommon to change caddies, coaches, psychologists or bring on a psychologist. We all know the business. I have no problem being fired. But I'm disappointed in the timing of it.' Woods' former swing coach, Hank Haney, hits the prevailing mood: 'I'm shocked. Steve is the best caddie I've ever seen. I can't believe that he got fired.'

Scott pounces. Williams becomes his full-time bagman. There is baggage, of course, and the inevitability of drama. At the 2002 Skins Game, Williams threw a camera into a pond at California's Landmark Golf Club when a photographer snapped a picture in the middle of Woods' backswing. At the 2004 US Open, he kicked the lens of a *New York Daily News* photographer. He's snatched a camera from a spectator, only to be informed it was an off-duty policeman.

Most caddies are seen and not heard. The mantra is to show up, keep up and shut up. Williams is carved from a different cloth. Put him in front of a microphone and take a deep breath. Asked about the frosty relationship between Woods and another great player, Phil Mickelson, at a charity event in New Zealand in 2008, Williams replies: 'I wouldn't call Mickelson a great player.' Why not? 'Because I hate the prick.'

In an interview the next day with the New Zealand-based *Star Times*, he adds: 'I don't partic-ularly like the guy. He pays me no respect at all and hence I don't pay him any respect. It's no secret we don't get along. I certainly didn't make the comments to a media person. I visit a lot of golf clubs and do a lot of speaking for charity and that is one of the questions I get asked the most: What is Tiger's relationship like with Phil Mickelson? I was simply honest and said they don't get along. You know what it's like. You're at a charity event and you have a bit of fun.'

One cup or two? Scott and Williams have their first win at the Bridgestone International at Firestone Country Club. Walking up the 18th fairway, Williams does what caddies never do. He smiles and waves to the gallery. His feud with Woods has dominated the week. They egg him on.

Way to go, Steve-ee!

Good job, Steve-ee!

Scott will beat Woods by eighteen shots.

Steve-ee!

Scott has a 7-iron to the green. He fancies the conservative option of aiming for the fat of the green. Williams tells him to go at the flagstick. Scott does as he's told. The ball travels 200-odd yards in the rainbow-arc shape of the Sydney Harbour Bridge. It lands ten feet from the stick, hops twice and rolls towards the hole as though it has been given a good and solid rap with a putter. It misses the hole by a whisker. Perfect. Williams high-fives Scott. He holds their grip before remembering it might be an idea to replace the divot.

Steve-ee!

He's only warming up. CBS commentator David Feherty has to grab a quick interview before the broadcast shuts down and America switches its attention to *60 Minutes*. Feherty interviews Scott. The Australian goes through his verbal motions. Stoked to win, and so forth. And then Feherty makes the snap decision to question the caddie. Again, this is unheard of. The New Zealander does more than go through the verbal motions, ignoring Feherty's softball questions to speak the truth. His truth. The next 101 seconds reveal a man with a tornado in his head.

Feherty: 'I tell you Stevie, for someone who's won seven times, I think you've won eight times now, is that right?'

Williams: 'Hey I've got to tell you David, I've been a caddy for 33 years, and that's the best week of my life. And I'm not joking. I'm never, ever going to forget that week. The people here this week have been absolutely unbelievable. And all the support from the people back in New Zealand, including my family—that's the greatest week of my life.'

Feherty: 'How is this different? I mean, you know, you've caddied for the best player in the world, without question. You've seen some of the greatest golf that's ever been played. To come out and get on with a youngster like this, it has to be a heck of a change but, I mean, you seem to be in your element still. I mean, with somebody who's not so much at the start of their career, but more of someone you can shape?'

Williams: 'David, it's like, you know—I caddy and I go racing. When I'm on the race track, the only place I'm interested in finishing is first. When I go to the golf course, it's the only place I'm trying to finish. Obviously it's a very tough game and you can't always win, but I'm a very confident front-runner. There were a lot of expectations today and I'd be lying if I said I wasn't a little nervous. Obviously Adam was leading the tournament and there's a lot being said all week. It's an incredible feeling to back it up. I always back myself, just like I do when I go racing. I'm a great front-runner when I go racing, and I feel like I'm a good front-runner when I'm caddying. I have great belief in myself but honestly, that's the best week of my life. I've been caddying for 33 years and that's 145 wins now and that's the best win I've ever had.'

Back to the commentary booth. The cameraman has slowly zoomed onto Williams' face. Interviewee barely takes a breath. Grey hair sticks from the sides of his Titleist cap. The crow's feet. The glazed and unblinking eyes.

'Wow,' says CBS anchorman Jim Nantz. 'That's all you can say.'

•• • ••

At Shanghai in November, after the second round of the HSBC Championships, players and caddies converge for their rowdiest night of the year, the Caddy Awards, a boozy banquet and piss-taking reflection on the past twelve months. One of the gongs is for Celebration of the Year. The room is buzzing because Williams will be the winner. The master of ceremonies asks Steve-ee about his comments to Feherty at Firestone. There are two versions of Williams' response. Firstly: 'I wanted to shove it up that black arsehole.' More commonly: 'It was my aim to shove it up that black arsehole.'

Either way, point taken. Nothing can be lost in translation.

It is believed Woods accused him of disloyalty in working with Scott. Everything at the Caddy Awards is supposed to remain at the Caddy Awards but British reporters returning from a night out of their own are told the anecdote by numerous caddies at the hotel bar. They print it the following day. 'Why would they do that?' says Williams. 'The whole thing was meant to be fun.' Another posting on his website: 'I apologize for comments I made last night at the Annual Caddy Awards dinner in Shanghai. Players and caddies look forward to this evening all year, and the spirit is always joking and fun. I now realize how my comments could be construed as racist. However, I assure you that was not my intent. I sincerely apologize to Tiger and anyone else I've offended.'

Scott is told by a member of the media pack that Williams should be fired. 'I disagree with that,' he says. 'Look, anything with Tiger involved is a story. I value Steve's contribution to my game and having him on the bag. While he's caddying for anyone, I hope he can caddie for me.' Scott is asked if Williams is racist. 'I think we all know that's not the case,' he says. 'Those things are not meant to go past that room. Obviously, somebody took it out and that's the way it goes. There's really no safe haven for what you say, and so you've got to be careful. I'm the guy stuck in the middle, but I don't really have a gripe with either guy. So it's for them to sort out between themselves. I don't think it should be awkward for me.'

Somewhere out there are recordings of the Caddy Awards of 2011. Attendees claim worse was said on the night, by other prominent figures, without being reported. 'When I finish my career, I'll document everything, why I have so much anger,' says Williams in the height of his damage control. The week after the Shanghai surprise, Woods, Williams and Scott gather in Sydney for the Australian Open.

'Obviously it was the wrong thing to say,' says Tiger. 'That's something we both acknowledge now. He did apologise. It was hurtful, certainly, but life goes forward. Steve is not a racist. It was just a comment that shouldn't have been made and one he wishes he didn't make.' Asked about his former caddy now being with Scott, Woods says: 'It was a difficult decision to go a different direction in my professional life. As far as personally, I don't know how it could have happened the way it did, but it did. And here we are.' Scott seeks only one form of repayment. Another set of eyes. One cup or two?

They're an entrenched partnership by the time the 2012 Open Championship at Royal Lytham and St Annes rolls around. The Masters or the Open? Take your pick. The manufactured attractiveness or the raw beauty of Britain? The howling winds. The driving rain. Certain layouts on the Open's roster resemble cow paddocks. But it has been kind to Australians. Peter Thomson landed the Auld Claret Jug five times. Norman's two majors were both at the Open. After his banner 63 at Royal St George's in 1993, he declared: 'I am not a person who boasts, but I'm in awe of myself in the way I hit the golf ball today. It was just perfect.' Scott can still recall nearly every shot of that round. 'I watched the lot of it,' he says. 'It was around the time that I stopped playing other sports and really wanted to be a golfer. To see him win that one really spurred me along. It's one of the most prestigious tournaments in the world and he played so pure. I would say that was a big part of an important time in my life, golf-wise.'

·· ● ··

Scott turns 32 on the eve of the 141st Open. Phil and Casie give him a golf bag. Williams delivers advice: play the first hole tomorrow as if it's the 72nd. Start with all guns blazing. Ignore the tradition among players of easing themselves into a major: the idea that you cannot win the tournament on the first day, but you can lose it. Scott throws a 64 on the table. The driving is impeccable. The short game is crisp. Go the broomstick. Royal Lytham has more than 200 bunkers. Scott avoids every last one of them. On the 18th green, he has a putt to be the first player in Open history to shoot a 62. Three-putt bogey. Boo the broomstick. He leads by three from the esteemed trio of Woods, Ernie Els and Rory McIlroy.

'I haven't achieved my goal of winning major championships,' he says. 'That's what I've dreamt of as a kid, and that's what I made my goals about when I turned pro. So I guess I haven't achieved my goals. It's been a good career but I still feel like I've got a lot to play for and a lot to achieve. Most guys like to judge their success on winning and I've won a couple of tournaments most years. It's a good habit to have, because it's getting harder and harder to win out here and I'm looking for another win this year, but I won't have achieved what I have always wanted to achieve until I win a major—or more.'

Then comes a second round of 67. A third-round 68 pushes him four shots ahead. Here we go. The floodgates. If Scott wins one major, he might win ten. He just requires the first push of encouragement. The invaluable validation. He leads Graeme McDowell and Brandt Snedeker. Els is six behind.

'I just need to do all the same stuff I've been doing that's been effective so far and it shouldn't really change just because it's Sunday,' Scott says before everything changes because it's Sunday. 'Obviously, there are nerves. There's a finish line out there somewhere but throughout my career, somehow, I've been able to handle that situation fairly well. I can't really explain what I feel. I do know it's a benefit to have a guy like Steve on the bag. He's an experienced caddie and we're getting on really well out there. He believes in the way I'm going about my business and at some point tomorrow, I'm sure there's going to be a time when I have to lean on him. He's going to have some great advice for me on how to tackle a certain situation.' One cup or two?

The big breakthrough. 'I certainly hope so,' says Scott. 'It would be incredible, but I don't even want to think about it. I'm just excited for what tomorrow holds. It's going to be an incredible experience, whatever happens. I truly believe that I can go out and play a great round of golf. If I do that, then I think that makes it pretty hard for anyone to catch me. It's fun to be in this position because it's what I've been practising for and we'll get to see if the practice pays off or not. That's all I can say at the moment. I've never teed off in the last group of the Open before so while I'm sure I'm going to be nervous, they're good nerves. I'm excited because I'm playing well.'

Restless sleep? 'I won't have a problem sleeping,' he says. 'Ask anyone who knows me. I can put in some hours.'

The first fourteen holes go to plan. Scott retains the four-shot lead. And then . . .

The 15th hole at Royal Lytham and St Annes: Bogey. The first flutter of anxiety. And then . . .

The 16th hole at Royal Lytham and St Annes: Great hole. Made famous by Seve Ballesteros when he lost his tee shot so far right in the final round of 1979 that his ball finished in the car park. He had spent most of the tournament rescuing his ball from hay fields, drop zones, grandstands and articles of women's clothing. Rule 24–2 states that cars are movable obstructions—unless the keys cannot be located, as was the case here. *Can the owner of such-and-such Audi please return to your car. Seve doesn't have a backswing.* Ballesteros receives a free drop. Ever the showman, he finds the green and snatches birdie. Scott has taken a more conventional route but dropped another shot. It is slipping.

The 17th hole at Royal Lytham and St Annes: Another bogey.

Not again.

The 18th hole at Royal Lytham and St Annes: Els has birdied two of the final four holes to be in the clubhouse on seven under. Scott has started the final day on eleven under. He needs a par for a playoff. Els retreats to the putting green. What is it with putting? Professionals take a million practice swings in their lifetimes. Greens, hotel rooms, airports and in their heads. And they always need one more. Els is torn.

'When Adam first went out on the European Tour as a kid, a few of the more seasoned hands really put their arm around him,' says Phil Scott. 'Thomas Bjorn was fantastic. He was just an awesome guy to Adam in those early years. When Adam won the Players, which is a long time ago now, Thomas had been in the first group on Sunday. But he stuck around and was in the locker room when Adam came in. Darren Clarke was really nice to him.

'I've never forgotten those days. None of it was interfering, it was more of who are you having dinner with tonight? Do you need a lift? They were just good guys, and Ernie was one of them. He really looked out for him. I think that's one of the nice things about golf. You might want to beat the guy's brains out on the course, but there's no reason you can't be a good bloke about it. Guys like Ernie made Adam feel comfortable. Obviously as life went by, some of those relationships continued and developed. Adam still catches up with Thomas and Darren, but he saw less of those guys once he went to America. He's spent a lot of time with Ernie over the years and they've become good mates. From day one, he has just been a super nice guy to Adam.'

Scott stares down the 18th fairway. The practice swing. A birdie to win. The decent drive, good contact. The smattering of applause. Scott looks pleased, but then the expression changes. A fairway bunker is coming into play. Not there. Anywhere but there. He throws his tee in disgust. Removes his glove, spins his 3-wood in his hands. Penny for his thoughts: Scott's ball has nestled close to the lip. The pot is 169 yards from the green. Disaster, this. Williams hands over a wedge. No stance for Scott. Such a desperately grim picture. All he can do is chip it out sideways. His left foot is on the downslope, level with his right knee. All so hard, majors. He steps away. Leans on his club and caddie. He knocks the ball sideways, a plume of sand chasing it, everything going up in a puff of smoke. He taps the sand from the soles of his shoes. Cleans his wedge. Puts it back in his bag. Still 150 yards to the hole. It's over. A superb third shot leaves a makable putt for par. It is not over. Scott wipes his brow and bites his lip and hitches his pants and then he crouches to study the line. *Clink*. Always the sound a putt makes. *Clink*. Slowly, slowly, to oblivion. Groan. It really is over. He shakes his head in furious disbelief. Out on the putting green, Els is told he is the new Open champion.

'Obviously I'm so happy that I've won,' he says. 'But I've been on the other end more times than I've been on the winning end and it's not a good feeling. I think Adam is a little bit different than I am. I've seen him in the scorer's hut and he seems okay. I said to him, "I'm sorry how things turned out." I told him that I've been there many times and you've just got to bounce back quickly. Don't let this thing linger. I feel for him, but thankfully he's young enough. He's 32 years old. He's got the next ten years when he can win more than I've won. I've won four majors now, and I think he can win more than that.'

Don't let the bastards get you down.

'It's tough,' says Scott. 'You don't want to sit here and have to—I can't justify anything that I've done out there. I didn't finish the tournament well today. But next time—and I'm sure there will be a next time—I can do a better job of it. Maybe it hasn't sunk in yet. Maybe there will be a bit more disappointment when I get home and kind of wind down. I've just walked off the course and there's a lot to digest. I feel fine at the moment. I'm a positive guy. I'm optimistic and I want to take all the good stuff that I did this week and use that for the next time I'm out on the course.'

The cruelty of sport.

'I had my daughter with me, and Brad—some relatives were really upset,' says Phil.

'I just wanted to keep a lid on it and make sure everyone was okay. My principal concern, of course, was how Adam was going to be. As it turned out, he was typical Adam. Sunday night was not a mausoleum at the house but irrespective of the circumstances, golf or anything else in life, you don't want to look on and watch your kid in trouble or hurting, do you? So it wasn't pleasant. It was okay, but it wasn't great. Hurting would be the honest answer to how I felt. You're hurting for someone else, aren't you? It's not going to affect my life, other than watching Adam and his sister unhappy.

'But at the end of the day it's a game, and you go into the game knowing that it's a game of chance. I'd been around golf my whole life, and I'd always taken the view that Adam had what it takes. It didn't matter what anyone else was saying. I watched Tom Watson be called a choker for years. You just know that if you're good enough to get up there, you're good enough to win. You just have to learn the extra bits. Learn how your own mind works. But of course he was cut up. His dream was to win those things, and he let one go. It's such a game of fine margins and sometimes it's not in your control, but that tournament was in Adam's control.

'What I really remember is how the last few holes seemed to go in a minute. As a golfer, it was interesting because it wasn't the classic pick it up, hit it out of bounds, make seven, and then you think there it is, it's gone. At 15, 16 and 17, they were just minor errors. At 16, you shouldn't hit it past the pin on that hole. Suddenly you hit it 40 feet past and you have the world's hardest putt coming back. Seventeen, you can't miss that green left. They played all week to hit it to the front right quadrant there. They were bad errors, but they were quite small. They're just the things that happen under the pump.'

Any solace in Els being the one to benefit?

'I felt like knee-capping him,' laughs Phil.

•• • ••

Scott licks his wounds at his home in Switzerland's Crans Montana, a ski resort boasting the Golf Club Crans-sur-Sierre, one of the most breathtaking layouts on the planet. Scott's neighbour beneath the Swiss Alps is Spanish enigma Sergio Garcia. Sophia Loren has owned a chalet overlooking the eighth green. Roger Moore has joined the neighbourhood. Given the setting, ridiculous is the notion of Scott having failed in this lifetime. Yet golfers are slaves to their results. Crans' locals mostly speak French, so no one can question him about the infamous Open collapse. If they are talking about it, he is blissfully unaware. He has company.

'We arrived on Monday,' says Phil. 'By Wednesday, he was definitely over the biggest hurt. He was genuinely pretty positive. You're never going to take the line that you've stuffed up and you're done. You're taking the line of hey, you only have to do an hour better. What has it shown? What do we know? It has shown that when you play, you can play better than anyone. So let's take that on. He was genuinely really good. The last four holes weren't rubbish. They just got a bit out of kilter. It was just the two of us in Switzerland and I was just a shoulder to lean on if he needed one. I was going somewhere else after the Open but I thought I'd go with him if he wanted me to. It ended up being a nice few days for us. We were on the course again by the Wednesday. On the practice facility at Crans, hitting balls. It was all about moving on.'

Scott ties for eleventh at the last major of the year, the PGA. His majors haul for 2012 is a tie for eighth at the Masters, 15th at the US Open, second at the British Open and his eleventh at Kiawah

Island. He wins the Australian Masters at Kingston Heath but his hunger is yet to be satisfied.

'I really have to focus on winning majors now for the rest of my career,' he says. 'At the end of the day, and Jack Nicklaus said it the other week on the Ryder Cup coverage, that's what a player is judged on—how many majors he wins. It's true. I feel like my best ten years are still coming up. There's no time to waste. Ten years goes by quick. My first ten did. The next ten should be my best because I feel like there's continued improvement and consistency, and it feels like I could have won two majors this year. I could have won three, if we throw in the US Open. It was a slow start there but I played so well for the last three-and-a-half rounds. It's all right there. I can see how close I am, and that's motivating.'

What of Lytham's lament? 'The Open showed me that I have the game to control a major championship from Thursday through to Sunday. For me to step up on the big stage and control the tournament for so long was something I had worked hard for. I don't look back on it that much because it was a disappointing result in the end, and you have to get on with it, but absolutely I will be better next time I put myself in that situation. I would be a fool not to have learned from what happened there but no, I don't think it's harmed me at all.'

He demolishes Kingston Heath with a closing 67 to win by four from Englishman Ian Poulter. Awesome. Terrific. But the defining image of 2012 is still Scott all Norman-esque on his haunches on the 18th green in the moment his par putt missed at Royal Lytham. He has apologised to his father for letting everyone down.

'I said, "Well, you haven't at all, Ad,"' says Phil.

'Initially, it was devastating,' says Malone.

'There was more an element of shock than anything else because he thought he had performed poorly. The week following the Open must have been tough. Just thinking, wow, how did that happen? It sort of got away from him a little bit but I remember saying when we got back to the house that Rory McIlroy let one slip through his fingers at the Masters, and he backed it up straight away with a win at the US Open. You have to just focus now and let's go perform at the PGA. He embraced that. He played well at the PGA, but then there's all that time before the Masters the next year. August until April. You have all that time to sit and reflect and think, okay, that was a great chance. If I keep putting myself in position, the door will open eventually. He put himself four shots ahead on the final day of a British Open and then held it until the final four holes. As ironic as it might sound, it gave him confidence. It wasn't one thing that happened over the last four holes but a slight accumulation of errors. What it confirmed to him is that he was good enough to win a major.'

No tantrums.

No passing of the buck.

'He has an amazing strength of mind,' says Malone. 'He can block things out and focus. I admire that in him. I don't think everybody would have reacted the way he did. The big thing was that he didn't lose the British Open through nerves or anxiety. It was just a series of errors that compounded. He said he felt very calm and in control. That's just his nature. One of Adam's better attributes, and it's the same for all those around him, is how realistic he is. They all keep it simple. In golf, it's easy when it's going your way. But what are you going to do when it gets tough? Because that's the measure of everything, isn't it? In life, when we're all rolling along and it's going our way, that's easy. But what happens when it gets tough? How are we going to react? Are we going to go in a corner and have a sulk or are we going to attack?'

Closing out the Australian Masters is therapeutic. 'I haven't been dwelling on what happened at the Open otherwise you'd never come back to the golf course, would you?' says Scott. 'It's kind of painful. But I'm trusting that my game is going to hold up. That I'm not going to get in my own way.' He contemplates the latest addition to his wardrobe and casts his mind towards Augusta and considers the possibility of turning his golden jacket to a Masters shade of green: 'Maybe I can . . .'

4

SNAPSHOTS

'While we may not have expected it originally, we have created a tournament of such importance that we are bound to see that it continues.'
Clifford Roberts

The Augusta National Golf Club is the grand cathedral of golf, but she is also the Fort Knox. There shall be no peeping through the trees for a glimpse of the place where the grass is greener. On a normal weekend, only twenty of the 300 members are likely to be having a whack. Eighty is considered heavy traffic. Washington Road veers off the Savannah River and leads to the brick wall . . . it is so quiet in here. None of the noise from town infiltrates the creaking, whispering grounds. This is where the most powerful men in America used to come to let the real world spin without them for a while. Now it is where the most powerful men in the world plus Condoleezza Rice and Darla Jones seek their sanctuary from dear suburbia.

Grease-monkey hamburger joints in town punctuate a gaudy scene that is far removed from the interior of the club and its sprawling, swooping grounds. Up hill and down dale. Peaks and valleys. Closed from the third week of May until mid-October, Augusta National has five primary events on the members' calendar. No guests or wives (or husbands) are welcome. There's the Masters itself. There's the Opening Party in October, the Governor's Party in November, the Jamboree in late March and the Closing Party in the third week of May. In the shadows of another Masters, when millions upon millions of dollars have been banked for another year, the members play their eighteen-hole competition to end the season. Two points for a birdie or better. One point for a par. Zero points for bogeys or worse. Some of the members adjourn to the Library for a whiskey and cigar. Others squeeze in another eighteen holes before dark. And then the course is closed for five months.

The Jamboree is the real hoot. Augusta's white scoreboards are in position for the Masters and the members use them for their own amusement. If chairman Billy Payne is winning the Jamboree, Billy Payne's name will be on top of the Masters leader board. And Billy Payne will be excited like a little kid. The Jamboree closes with a short film from the chairman. There are scenic shots. Tributes to deceased members. The original chairman, Clifford Roberts, once showed a clip of himself walking across the pond at the 16th after hitting a hole-in-one. A small bridge had been built just below the surface to give the desired effect. His caddie has been ordered to fall into the water. Further footage has shown Roberts chasing players off the course in a bear suit. In another skit, he's sung to a rubber ducky. 'Well, Mr Roberts felt . . .' remains a popular refrain from the six chairmen to have followed him.

Members Only.

The Library hosts the socialising, card games and telling of tales, tall and true. High-stakes gambling is not viewed favourably. Anything frowned upon at Augusta, the official word is that it's not viewed favourably. Membership may be terminated as a result of big-money wagers. The termination will only become known when the member's invoice simply fails to arrive in the post the following spring.

'There's a great story about gambling and a guy who was the chairman two chairmen ago,' says Newton. 'He was six foot six, used to wear the big Texan hat. This other guy was a new member coming in. New members have to play with the chairman in their first round at the club. Having been accepted, if he gets knocked back by another member in the first month, he's out. The new member gets on the first tee and says to this chairman, would you like to play for a few dollars? The chairman says, "In my group, we play ten, ten and ten." Meaning ten dollars the front nine, ten dollars the back nine and ten dollars for the winner over the eighteen holes. The bloke said that's a bit weak, isn't it? The Texan said that's the rules. So this new member has pounded the chairman about how little they were playing for. They get in the clubhouse afterwards and he's still on about it. The Texan says to him, tell me how much you're worth. The bloke says, well, at the last count it was $119 million. There was a deck of cards on the table on the bar. The big fella says I'll cut you for it. He didn't get any more cheek out of him.'

The Library displays the first watercolour sketch of the course by the architect, Alister MacKenzie. And a portrait of Clifford Roberts by President Eisenhower. See the pull of Roberts? The President drew *him*.

··•··

Masters week: pubs and restaurants are crammed to overflowing. Touts are camped in their motorhomes. The triumph and despair. The magic of it all. The back nine on a Sunday, the back nine on a Sunday, the back nine on a Sunday. All rather beautiful. The charmed life. The pursuit of perfection. The eccentricities. Let the privileged be privileged. The elegance and attractiveness. The exclusivity. Norman ended up receiving a matter-of-fact letter from Hootie Johnson saying that regretfully, a playing invitation could no longer be extended. It was that black and white. Norman was invited to attend as a guest. He declined. He had given Scott an introduction in the first of the snapshots in the wannabe Norman's scrapbook.

··•··

Snapshot #1. 'It was very peaceful out there,' says Scott of his first sighting of Augusta. 'I walked out of the clubhouse and I couldn't believe how open the area was in front of us. The 18th green and the ninth green, and then down in the valley, which I believe was the old range where they used to warm up a long time ago. It was such a big, open area, and I was surprised by that. I played a practice round with Greg Norman, and we poured some water on the 16th green at the top, and it rolled off the green. The water trickled down. It didn't sink into the green at all. That was pretty scary.'

Embarrassing moments while acclimatising? 'Probably putting off the 17th green in my first year, on the Sunday. There's been a few. Not getting up a slope and having it roll back past where I started from, stuff like that. My first year here was the last time Greg played, and I got to spend a couple of days with him, talking to him a bit about Augusta . . . I was actually staying at his house one year when he was playing in the tournament. This was before I was in it, and I look back on a practice round we had as one of my fondest memories in the game. He pointed out little nuances of the golf course and ways to tackle a few different holes. For me to be out here, playing with my hero and seeing everything about the course that I had watched on television, to be playing with Greg Norman at Augusta, that was pretty special.'

The tie for ninth on his spectacular debut has been followed by four years of aggravation, of missing the cut and/or failing to crack the top twenty. 'My first year here, I was thinking, what's the big deal?' he says. 'I heard people talking about the tricky course—what are they talking about? But then I got a few slaps in the face. Certainly there has been a developing level of comfort over the years, but experience is only part of it. You still have to hit the shots. You still have to execute. If you have a few tough rounds out here, and I have, it can get away from you pretty quickly. You can actually feel a little embarrassed because it looks so ugly.

'That's what this course can do. It can break your confidence quickly, and it's not a good feeling. It took me a while to bring my game and confidence back here after the first year. I didn't think the course never suited me or anything like that. It was more that I was lost as to why I wasn't playing my best golf at any of the majors. My record here wasn't horrible, but I was never really in contention, always the middle of the pack. It took me a long time to figure out why I wasn't bringing my best game to the majors but the week after or the week before, I could win on tour. I'd done that a fair few times and it was hard to figure out. Maybe I was just a slow learner.'

.. ● ..

Snapshot #2. American journalists wait until 2007 to request an interview with Scott. Only then is he regarded as a contender. 'Well, actually, it's my first time in the media centre here in Augusta, and that's a little disappointing considering I've been here five years,' Scott grins. Gentle probing. For an Australian, what does the tournament mean? 'It's probably the Holy Grail of golf right now,' he says. 'It's hard to qualify, so just getting to play here is an achievement in itself. I certainly dream of winning it and for any Australian, it would be indescribable. We're a strong sporting nation and we push our athletes hard, and it's one of the things we haven't won. It will happen: one good round might be all it takes. One good round and an Aussie can earn this championship.'

Run the rule over your first five years? 'Well, the first year was good, played well. Maybe I didn't know what I was getting myself into. After that I played a little too defensively and worried too much about the results of bad shots. Last year, though, I took the attitude of playing a little more aggressively and free-wheeling it a bit. I didn't play great, but I certainly saw something in just going out there and playing golf and not worrying so much. I just didn't execute last year, but I want to keep taking that same free spirit out there.'

He's asked for the first (and not the last) time by an international pensmith about Norman. He never seems to tire of the topic. 'I certainly was attracted to his style of golf,' he says. 'I grew up modelling myself on him in every way. I was swinging like him with a big, you know, whip over the shoulder and bounce-it-off-the-back follow-through. He played really aggressive golf. I think that won him 80-something tournaments around the world and it probably cost him a few tournaments, too. I try to take the good out of the way he played. There's a right time to be aggressive and a wrong time. It's about controlling the aggression. Knowing when to hit away from a flag because it's not the right time to get after it.'

More directly, when are you going to win a major? 'I think I'm definitely more patient with myself than other people are,' he says. 'I've learned a lot from Geoff Ogilvy the last couple of years, actually. It's interesting. We talk a lot and we're good friends. I started playing majors pretty early in my career compared to him. He was a much more mature player when he started and had a lot more self-belief than I did when I was younger. Geoff's mind-set is that majors are the easiest tournaments to win. When I was twenty, I thought I had no chance, even though I dreamed about it. I thought they were the hardest tournaments by far but just feeding off Geoff's mind-set has helped in the last year.'

How (on earth) does Ogilvy reason that majors are the most simple to win? Jack Nicklaus, the G.O.A.T. (Greatest Of All Time), won eighteen majors. But he was runner-up in nineteen. He played 163, which means he lost 145. That's 48 years, from the 1957 US Open to the 2005 British Open at St Andrews, of mostly being defeated. 'Well, Geoff explains it like it's a matter of survival,' says Scott. 'He says you just have to hang around. You don't have to do anything that special for three days. Hang around and then Sunday is the day where you really find out what's happening. Fifty per cent of the field in contention on Sunday goes the wrong way. Only a few guys are normally going the right way. Geoff feels like you don't have to shoot twenty under. And it's not just a putting competition. It's about being solid and keeping yourself in contention. And look what happened to him last year. He hits a great chip on 17, gets up and down and everyone stumbles over the line. Geoff's in the clubhouse and he wins the US Open. That's not a very clear explanation, but his mind-set is that so many people are beaten before they even start, and that was me when I was younger. I didn't have the self-belief that I would be there on Sunday.'

Thought you had to do something heroic? 'Absolutely, yeah,' he says. 'Whereas now, I'm a different golfer. I can get myself into position for Sunday and then on Sunday, okay, it's going to be a tough day out there. But it can happen without any real heroics. It's the mental approach to the majors. I felt like I had to play better than I'd ever played before to win one of them. That's what Geoff talks about. He thinks he doesn't have to play 110 per cent to win the US Open. He putted great that week he did win it, obviously, but if you ask him, he'd probably say he was at about 80 per cent and not entirely happy with everything. He was smart, stayed within himself all week, and at the end of the week he was on top.'

Annoyed by not winning a major yourself yet? 'Not at all,' says Scott. 'If every other 26-year-old was out here winning majors, I'd be annoyed, but that's not the case. It's something that I would like to happen sooner rather than later, but I think you've got to be a little patient with this.'

Scott is 27th in 2007. Humbug. The following year, as if Scott has become Sideshow Bob, as if he is no longer being taken seriously as a golfer, the most interest is in the Golf Channel naming him the sexiest player of all time. As if it matters. As if questions about it were to be taken seriously. 'I guess I take it as a compliment,' yawns Scott. 'But I don't get a green jacket for it.'

·· ● ··

Snapshot #3. A second-round 75 kills him in 2010. Eighteenth. Exasperating. 'It is when you putt like a moron out there,' he says. 'That's the worst putting display of my life. I hit the ball great but it's hard to have a good score when you're putting like that. Four three-putts, that's just ridiculous. And I missed every other opportunity I had. It's frustrating. It's a shame to play good and then putt like that.' The anger! A first time for everything. 'Confidence is shot,' he says. 'That's what happens when you have a few too many putts.' What happened to the drive on the 13th? 'I just pulled it,' he says curtly. And it went in the azaleas? 'Yeah. You managed to pick my one bad shot there, didn't you? It just feels like I have to go out and play perfect to have a good score and that's not a very fun way to play. You can't throw shots away here. I need to be making putts from ten feet and in—and I just stood there and missed all day. So it's annoying—but it's a work in progress.'

•• • ••

Snapshot #4. Equal second with Jason Day in 2011. The impeccable final round of 67. But then Charl Schwartzel's four straight birdies in sight of the podium. 'I don't think I can ask for anything more,' says Scott. 'I had a putt at it on the last, and it was kind of an outside chance, and it wasn't my best putt, but when someone finishes like Charl did, what can you do?' Incredible vibe. The roars and groans of the patrons from all parts of the course. 'I was looking at the leader boards until the last couple of holes,' says Scott. 'It's hard to not hear all the stuff going on. You can tell when guys are making moves. I knew I was leading after I birdied 16, but I could hear right behind me what Charl was doing. That's my first time in that atmosphere on a Sunday, and it was fantastic. I just want to keep putting myself in the mix from here. Obviously I can't control what Charl did. When someone birdies the last four holes at the Masters and he's around the lead—there's nothing I can do about that. To be right in the mix here is everything I've dreamed of and that was another incredible finish. It's amazing what happens at this place.'

He sounds flat.

'I'm not flat. But I held the lead with a few holes to go. It's just a shame I didn't get it done in the end. I walked to the 17th tee with a one-shot lead and parred the last two holes, which I thought was pretty good on those holes. Normally that would be enough, but what Charl did was extraordinary.'

Now he sounds disappointed.

'I'm not disappointed with anything I did. I think there was a certain level of maturity in my game. It was really my first opportunity to win a major and I guess there was ten years' experience in there somewhere. It's not just straight down the fairway, straight on the green kind of stuff at this course. There's the extreme undulation and movement. I think before it was a bit of a lottery, whether my game would show up. I think now I know it's going to be there.'

Schwartzel!

'Look, I hit one bad shot on the Sunday, and that was on 15,' says Scott. 'I blocked a 5-iron right and ended up making par. It's hard to be critical of that. I stood up on the next and hit a great 7-iron to a foot or so and made a birdie. It's hard to change anything because in the end, I was two shots behind, and I can't find two more shots out there. I didn't birdie the par fives on Sunday, but I birdied some other holes which I wouldn't expect to. I was just beaten fair and square. It was just good golf from Charl. Great golf. I don't feel like I lost.'

Cursed!

'I think it makes the story a little juicier,' he says. 'There's another line you can put in your story: Australia came second again. One year someone is going to get across the line and it's going to be incredible for them. Not only would you be the

Masters champion but in Australia, there would be that little asterisk next to your name for being the first we ever had.'

·· • ··

Snapshot #5. Great expectations in 2012. Scott begins with a 75. Pack up and go home. Gotta lose eleven to win one? He ends with a 66. Finishes eighth. What a waste. He aces the 16th on Sunday: too little, too late. 'It was just a 7–iron, a little 7–iron,' he deadpans. 'I hit a nice shot, so it went in.' Whatever. The joy is fleeting. Top ten. Big deal. 'I was playing well but it's just . . .' He wants more. 'It's such a hard golf course to . . .' Words fail him.

'It's just not easy to put it all together,' he says. 'One hole can be so crucial. I'm really happy to leave with my best round ever at Augusta, but I'm a little disappointed that I couldn't put it together earlier in the week. I really feel comfortable here now. I feel like I have these rounds in me, but I didn't have good pace on the greens and therefore I hit a lot of good putts that didn't go in. And then I hit a few bad ones. It's costly. We get to the end and I'm left thinking about my three–putts. I look around and I'm not that far behind the leaders, and

I know I could have been right there. That's the positive. I have to take that as a positive. And then I have to figure out how to get out of the gate better on the Thursday so I don't have to work so hard to get back in the tournament. I wouldn't say I have regrets. If you are living with regrets then you are going to really struggle out here on the tour. You just have to somehow take it for what it is. For me now, I just have to work a bit harder. That's the only answer. I'm doing all the right things, but it just didn't happen again. Somehow I have to make it happen. I have to be a bit harder and tougher on myself when I'm teeing off on the Thursday.'

The roar on 16 while Scott's ball has scurried to the hole has been deafening down in the valley, but it's been a year after he needed it most. 'It was massive down there,' he says. 'I hit a shot that was feeding down there last year, too. It just missed. I would have liked to switch them.'

There will be a time and place.

5

WHERE THE GRASS IS GREENER

'It's just a paradise.'
Gary Player

Paradise is where a mutual friend of Bobby Jones and
Clifford Roberts, Thomas Barrett Jr, recommended
a 365-acre property called Fruitland Nurseries as
a potential site for a golf course in the early 1930s.
Where Jones exclaimed upon his first sighting:
'Perfect! And to think this ground has been lying
here all these years waiting for someone to come
along and lay a golf course on it.' Where Jones and
Roberts paid $70,000 for the acreage. Where Jones
helped design the course with Scottish architect Dr
Alister MacKenzie.

Where Jones decided on the name of Augusta National. Where the inaugural event was staged in 1934, two months after the death of MacKenzie. It was won by Horton Smith. 'To me, the Augusta National course has character, individuality and personality,' he said. 'It's one of the few courses that really presents two games on most every hole—a game to reach the greens and another to figure the ever-challenging contours after reaching the green.'

It's where the event was originally called the Augusta National Invitation Tournament because Jones thought 'The Masters' sounded too immodest. Where the original title existed for five years until Jones relented and agreed to Roberts' request for a grander title. Jones played twelve times without finishing better than 13th. Said Jones in his book *Golf is My Game*, 'I think the tournament is now quite well entitled to be called the Masters, because it has continued to assemble those who are entitled to be called masters of the game; and although we must admit that the name was born of a touch of immodesty on the part of Cliff, yet it has only attached itself to the tournament because of the approval and adoption of the name by the newspaper boys who followed it.'

Paradise is where, in 1935, Gene Sarazen holed a 4-wood from 235 yards for an albatross on the par-five 15th. Sarazen's caddie was called 'Stovepipe' for the old silk top hat he wore. Sarazen trailed Craig Wood by three shots, and he debated with Stovepipe: 3-wood or 4-wood? The old hesitant feeling. 'I rode into the shot with every ounce of strength and timing I could muster,' Sarazen said. Paradise is where the Masters' archive states: 'The ball took off as if shot from a cannon, flying on a line, barely 30 feet high. It landed on the front portion of the putting surface, hopped forward and rolled directly into the cup. In just one swing, Sarazen had made up the three strokes separating him and Wood. The modest gallery behind the green erupted in applause; soon thousands scurried down from the clubhouse to follow Sarazen over the final three holes. Needing to par to tie with Wood, he managed to do just that. The toughest of those pars came at the last, where, playing into a slight wind from the left, Sarazen reached for his 4-wood once again. His shot came to rest 30 feet past the hole and he two-putted for four.

'The 36-hole playoff was held the next day in unusually chilly weather. Both men went out in even-par 36 on the opening nine, but Sarazen built a four-shot lead by lunch. He gained another stroke on Wood in the afternoon to win the tournament going away—a magisterial victory set in motion by what is, to this day, celebrated as the "shot heard 'round the world". Paradise is where Sarazen declared: "That double eagle wouldn't have meant a thing if I hadn't won the playoff the next day. The aspect I cherish most is that both Walter Hagen and Bobby Jones witnessed the shot."'

·· ● ··

Down Magnolia Lane, where the tree branches are extended arms, bent at the elbow, offering a handshake. Where the clubhouse is a little house on a prairie. Where the noise and junk from the bars and hamburger joints of Washington Road cease to exist. Where commentators have to mind their P's and Q's. 'Jack Whitaker was the head of CBS's sports commentating,' says Newton. 'He had the job of doing the 18th hole at Augusta. I think it was 1971 or so, the year Jack Nicklaus won his first Masters. This Jack Whitaker said, "It's a wonderful scene around the 72nd hole as the mob rushes for position around the green. Jack Nicklaus needs two putts to win his first Masters . . ." Something like that. At the end of the telecast, he was told that Clifford Roberts wanted to see him. Clifford said to Jack Whitaker, "Listen, Jack. The term 'mob' is synonymous with the mafia, not golf galleries at the Masters. Your services are no longer required." They replaced him with a guy called Vin Scully. Vin got laryngitis. CBS went to Augusta and pleaded with Roberts to let Jack Whitaker back. Years later, there was Gary McCord on the 17th hole. Gary said, "This is a great shot coming in here". It hit the green and just kept rolling to the back. Gary McCord says, "I don't know what's wrong with this 17th green, but it looks like it's been top-dressed with bikini wax." He was gone, too, and he's never been back.'

Eisenhower Tree is the meeting place for members to parade their single-vented, lightweight, single-breasted jackets, the Masters logo on the front buttons and cuffs. In a thick veil of fog at 7.45 a.m. on Thursday, 9 April, Nicklaus, Arnold and Player, with their combined 233 years and thirteen Masters triumphs, perform the ceremonial tee-off. 'It's just a paradise,' says Player. 'It's so beautiful. When I walk through Magnolia Lane every year, I just say a little prayer of thanks. It's a special place.' Says Palmer: 'As far as I'm concerned, there will never be another tournament to equal it.' Nicklaus recalls beating Norman in '86 at the ripe old age of 46.

'I don't even know why I was playing,' he says. 'I had sort of finished my career. But I just happened to like playing golf and I wanted to be part of it. I didn't know what was going to happen but I started hitting the ball well, and I started putting well with that big putter I had, and I ran the tables in the last round. I started making birdies and all of a sudden I remembered how to play. I remembered the feeling of being in contention. I remembered the feeling of how to control your emotions and how to enjoy the moment. I had my son, Jack, caddying for me. I was standing there on 15, and I said, "How far do you think a three will go here?" And I said, "I don't mean the club." I was serious yet I was kidding.

'I made eagle. At 16, I hit a 5-iron in there, that was 175 yards, and I just put a soft 5-iron in the air. I remember when I hit the shot, I looked down and Jack said, "Be right, be right." And I said: "It is." It was the cockiest remark I ever made, but it was in fun and jest—even though I knew the shot was right. I just remembered how to play and what to do coming down the stretch. I remember stopping about halfway down the 15th fairway, and I looked around me, and I saw all these people excited and having fun. I thought this a lot of times in my career: this is what I'm out here for. This is what I'm supposed to be doing. This is why I'm having so much fun. That's when I made the little remark to Jack: how far does a three go here? The game doesn't have to be so serious that you strangle yourself.'

Palmer, Player and Nicklaus poke their drives up the middle. Palmer hits first. Crisp white shirt and red sweater. Followed by Player in his head-to-toe black and then Nicklaus in a tan cardigan. 'I wish it was a little foggier,' says Palmer for a laugh. Player cuts one up the middle. Nicklaus is a little left, but on the fairway. All have hit 3-woods. Nicklaus has teed up his ball, stepped away a few paces and flexed his club behind his back. 'Do we get practice swings?'

The line of his ceremonial drive is identical to his first drive here in 1959. 'The nerves are about making contact with the golf ball because it makes diddley-darn where it goes,' says Nicklaus. 'We're just lucky we all hit 'em. Arnold made good, solid contact. He was absolutely delighted. Gary, I don't know how he hit his. I pulled mine a little bit but they'll find 'em, chase 'em, bring 'em back and do something with 'em.'

They retreat to the clubhouse for breakfast. Who's going to win it? Ignore the obvious answer in Tiger Woods. Use some imagination. 'I haven't looked at the field,' jokes Nicklaus. 'Who's playing?' High spirits. 'Obviously Tiger is playing very well. I'm delighted to see Rory go well again. Phil always plays well. Keegan Bradley has had a good year up to this point. Dustin Johnson hits it nine miles.' Last but not least: 'Adam Scott always plays well here.'

Five hours after the ceremonial duties have been performed, Adam Scott begins his twelfth Masters campaign with Angel Cabrera and Sergio Garcia. Want another omen, saints? He birdies the first, stiffing an 8-iron from a fairway trap. How does it feel to tee off on the opening day at Augusta National Golf Club? Scott marvels at the hammering of nerves and the surreal sensation of being unable to keep his feet on the ground. The emotion of strolling off the first tee and straight into the oil painting. The grass is dyed thick green and the bunkers are impossibly white. 'You're floating,' he says.

·· ● ··

Scott and Els have arrived in Augusta on a private jet in March for a research and destroy mission. Eighteen holes to whet the appetite. 'Would they have chatted on the way around about the strategy? Of course,' says Phil Scott. 'Would Ernie have said this is how you play Augusta? I'm not sure that's right. The fact is Ernie and Adam are very good mates, and Ernie couldn't be nicer to Adam. He always has been. That's why we know Ernie's emotion after the Open last year was genuine. He really did feel it. He's a good guy and they would have enjoyed that day at Augusta.'

The Scotts have rented a house a stone's throw from the club. Phil, Brad Malone and Steve Williams are sharing the lodgings with Jay. Their chef from Las Vegas. 'He's a fantastic guy,' says Phil. 'Adam gets him to every major because at the majors, obviously they rent a house and it's a lot easier to have your own chef than worrying about what you're going to do for food. He's just awesome. Great fella with a great personality. He understands Adam and all the others that stay. He knows what they like and understands the timing of everything. You don't have to tell him. He can look at the draw and work it out for himself. It's just a terrific atmosphere.'

Scott plays practice rounds with Germany's former world No. 1 Martin Kaymer on Saturday and Sunday. Then on the Monday and Tuesday, he's in cahoots again with Els and Louis Oosthuizen, the South African who won the 2010 British Open at St Andrews. 'When Ernie walked off the course, he walked past me and said: "Your boy is playing awesome",' recalls Malone. 'He said, "Your boy is striking it."'

All Scott's houses are in order. The rented premises and the golf game. 'Everything feels like it's in good shape,' he says. 'I feel like I'm here and ready to compete. The last couple of years have certainly shown dramatic improvement in my results in majors. All of the boxes are ticked and it's down to execution. A couple of times already I felt like I executed well enough to win but it just didn't happen. That could be just golf or it could be something else that I haven't quite got yet, I don't know. But I'd like to think I'm doing the right things and I'm going to get myself in that position again a couple of times this year in the big ones. I've developed a real level of comfort with this golf course in the last three years so for me, I say quietly confident, that I believe I can make it happen.'

A lightning start to match Royal Lytham's will help. 'But you can't just plan a hot start,' he says. 'I think I've said in the past that those first six or seven holes are probably the most difficult on this golf course. You start out on Thursday with the nerves on the first tee and then it's about getting yourself to calm down. They're very demanding holes and if you can just play your way through there, then you set yourself up for some good opportunities. I'd be happy with just a solid start.'

In his next breath, though, he says: 'I had a slow start here last year, so I'm looking for something a little more solid this time. Not just going out on the back foot. I really changed my mind-set to start the Open Championship on the front foot and switch on from the first hole, and not have a couple of early bogeys that end your momentum or stop you from playing as well as you can. Bad starts are hard to recover from in majors. The confidence can take a little hit and you can doubt yourself and then you're exposed on these tough courses.'

Scarred by Lytham? Scott Hoch, Jean Van de Velde . . . the list is long of those to never recover from blowing a major.

'Well, I can only speak for myself, and I don't

think about it that much,' he says. 'You've just got to get on with it. That was the nice thing for me, referring to the Open last year—I was playing a week later and I was back out there and the following week was another major. There was no time to sit and feel sorry for myself that I didn't win, because I was trying my hardest to win the next one, the PGA. At the end of last year I had a chance to win a tournament in Australia and I managed to do it. That was good because obviously you don't want to make it a thing that you struggle to close out a golf tournament. That's never really been the case with me but the more you're up there, the more you're going to win and the more you're going to lose, and that's something that you have to deal with. I didn't dwell on it at all. All I'm trying to do is play my best golf. It's pretty simple.'

He could hardly have chosen a more comfortable pairing than Cabrera and Garcia if he was allowed to pick the names out of the hat himself. 'You need a little bit of winner's luck here,' he says. 'I think everyone who wins the tournament has it, but it's not something you can make happen. I guess it just happens and when it's meant to be, it's meant to be. You know, Charl had an amazing couple of shots early in his final round, and then he produced incredible golf at the end of 2011. So it just happens. I don't know, that stuff, you can't control it. I think the golfing gods sort all those things out.'

Woods is the raging favourite. He's returned to the world No. 1 ranking and dominated the regular tour with wins in California, Arizona and Florida, but Scott believes the aura of invincibility is a relic of the past. 'We all know what he's capable of doing,' says Scott. 'He's got the runs on the board and he's always a threat at any golf tournament. But he's far from just running away with it at the moment. He's returned to No. 1 but that's just a number. I mean, there are so many guys playing well, it's not a foregone conclusion. The biggest thing is that some of the guys weren't out here when he was in that space where he was dominating everyone. They never saw that and so they don't know of him really doing it. Or they haven't actually seen him at that level he was before. That's the difference. I think he'd have to put the runs on the board again to get back to that.'

Nicklaus has never spoken at length with Woods. Professional jealousy is another form of curse. Woods' pursuit of Nicklaus' record of eighteen majors is stalled on fourteen. It seemed a fait accompli after Torrey Pines, but he is yet to win a major since. Time has always been on his side but now he's 37. Nicklaus' benchmark of eighteen might just survive.

'I never really had a conversation with Tiger that lasted more than a minute or two—ever,' says Nicklaus. 'He's stayed away from me from a conversation standpoint. Never had a conversation on the Masters in general. I've said, "Hello, how are you doing? Nice playing this year. You've played very well." End of conversation. People ask me, "Has Tiger ever talked to you about his record?" Never one word.' Not that Nicklaus is offended: 'He's got his own focus on what he does, and I respect that. I respect when somebody is involved in their deal. They concentrate on what they do and not what you did. That's okay. It's not my position to go talk to him about it. I wouldn't intrude on that. I asked him when he came to Florida if he wanted to come to The Bear's Club, but he stayed away from it. He didn't want to intrude where I was. He never told me why, but other people told me, "He says he didn't feel comfortable being there where I was because that was a record he was trying to break." I said, "I don't care about that. We'd like to have you if you want to play and be part of it." I'd include him in everything.'

·· ● ··

And On the First Day. Scott's opening tee shot finds a fairway bunker. Trouble. He nearly holes his 8-iron before tapping in his gimmee birdie. So much for the toughest hole on the course. Then comes a bogey at the second as though the shock of his whirlwind start has disturbed the equilibrium. An unsightly six, and the rousing beginning has gone to waste. Another birdie on the third and then another at the eighth, his shoulder to the wheel by now, a precise chip allowing an accomplished four. He treads through a tidy back nine of eight pars and a birdie on the 15th for an opening round of two-under 70. Less than a barn-burning statement of intent, but a dignified beginning.

'It's a great start,' he declares. 'It was a beautiful day. I mean, it doesn't get any better than today. I think it was really great for scoring conditions. We're seeing lots of good scores to start the week so I think that I'm happy with where I'm at. It's a start. I hit a great shot out of the fairway trap on 1, gave it straight back on the second—just had a little brain fade and then back to business. I played how I expected to. I could have created a couple more chances, but I didn't get very greedy with my irons so I didn't leave myself a lot of great chances. Just got to keep in touch again tomorrow. If I can stay three back or improve, that's a good spot going into the weekend.'

Garcia rips through a round of six-under-par 66 to share the lead. His surge is unexpected. Garcia regards the whole Augusta thing as a crock. His first question at the press conference is: 'Thought you hated it here?' Which deserves to be ranked alongside an American reporter once asking the generously proportioned Eduardo Romero: 'Why exactly do they call you The Cake?' And when Sandy Lyle was asked, 'What do you think of Tiger Woods?' He replied: 'Not sure I've ever played that course.' Garcia replies: 'It's obviously not my most favourite place. Let's enjoy it while it lasts.'

Garcia's blitzkrieg gives him a share of the lead with an unexpected figure, Marc Leishman, a burly sort of bloke from the Warrnambool club on the Great Ocean Road in Australia. He's ranked 108th in the world. He has fought illness and been on antibiotics since becoming sick around the time he was playing four-ball worst-ball matches with his father, Paul, during the Christmas break. The fatigue has made him unable to play more than nine holes at a time in practice. But on the eve of the Masters, on an otherwise nondescript Wednesday afternoon fit for casual strolls along the boardwalk framing the Savannah, Leishman decides he might wander out and have one last look at the back nine. He's stridden into the twilight zone and birdied the 10th. Amen Corner has given him birdie, birdie, eagle in an hour-long burst that proves he can dominate the course when the stars align and the antibiotics kick in. Between the azaleas and the pines and dogwoods, on a course so prim and proper that every last blade of grass is standing to attention, Leishman realises there is little to fear. He's one of four Australians in the field. The others are Scott, Jason Day and John Senden, and he is top of the pile on the Thursday night.

··●··

Leishman had a golf club in his hand from the day he could walk. His grandfather bought a house opposite Warrnambool golf course, dug holes in the lawn and offered his grandson 50 cents for every hole in one. The little Leishman had more 50 cent coins than he knew what to do with. In grade three at Warrnambool West Primary School, he told his teacher he was going to be a professional golfer. His parents still have a report card from his teacher: 'Keep up the good work and good scores (golf).'

He has burst to prominence with a second to Tiger Woods at the BMW Championship at Cog Hill in 2009. He earns the PGA Tour rookie of the year award. He debuts at the Masters in 2010, shortly before he is to marry Audrey Hills. The honeymoon is planned for Hawaii and guests begin arriving in the lead-up to the Masters, congregating at the home he has rented in Augusta, turning his Masters debut into an early celebration for the nuptials.

Walking the fairways, trying to fight the feeling he has stepped into a movie scene, memories flood back of the folkloric moments he has seen on television: Ian Woosnam winning in 1991; Mize's chip; Fred Couples' ball staying out of Rae's Creek in 1992. He plays like a man distracted for a simple enough reason: he is a man distracted. 'We had a lot of people who were over here for the wedding,' says his father, Paul. 'It turned into a bit of a party, not for Marc but the rest of the people there. It wasn't ideal. When we reflect on it now, we did it all wrong. This year is a lot different.'

On the first practice day, Leishman has quit after seven holes. 'I just felt like crap, pretty much,' he says. 'I had some sort of viral infection. I was coughing all week and not feeling great. I'd already been sick for about two months. We couldn't work out what it was. We went to the doctor and they put me on some stuff. It was like a bad cold that wouldn't go away. It sapped all my energy.'

Audrey Hills, which Sandy Lyle might confuse for the name of a golf course in the general vicinity of Tiger Woods, has caddied for him in the par three tournament. And then came his revelatory back nine in practice with Swede Henrik Stenson. 'I birdied 10, 11, 12 and then eagled 13—I had a pretty crazy few holes,' he says. 'I think it made me realise the course is gettable. You can make birdies out there if you hit good shots. On the other hand, I know how it can get up and bite you really quickly if you hit bad shots. Even if you're hitting good shots, if you miss it by ten feet you can end up in a terrible position.

'I think the big help was two or three years ago when I went there the first time, I realised there were some shots that I couldn't hit. I didn't have the shot—the big hook with the driver or 3-wood, I didn't have that. I've been working on that since the last Masters so I would be ready when I got in it again. There's a lot of holes where you have to hit it round corners like 10, 13 and 14 with the hook. Then I knew how sharp my short game had to be. I had been doing a lot of work on that in the month or so leading up. I was just working on the right things and practising smart, knowing what was coming up. I wanted to play really well here. I wanted it to all come together.'

Leishman bogeys the first from a hooked drive off the tee. Nerves? 'I don't shake or anything,' he says. 'Just over the ball, you're just, maybe your arms feel a bit light or something.' He recovers with birdies on 3 and 8. And then bang, bang, bang, bang and bang: birdies on 10, 13, 14, 15 and an enormous putt for one last birdie on 16. 'I don't know how far that was, but it was in a different postcode,' says Leishman. 'It just happens when you have a good day, occasionally, and you have to make the most of it.' Two pars to bring it home and Leishman is signing off on a 66.

'It's Augusta,' he says. 'It's at the same place

every year. You know every hole. It's so green and the flowers are out. It just looks unbelievable on TV. You think you're never going to get there. Growing up, I didn't think I would. Then all of a sudden you get here and it's better than you ever thought it could be, better than you thought anywhere could be. It's an unbelievable place. The British Open is obviously one of the ones we want to win but growing up in the Norman era, watching him at the Masters every year, I think that's why we all want to win the Masters. It's a different style of golf. If I had to pick one it would definitely be the Masters. Every kid wants to be here. The first time a few years ago, I was like a bit of a deer in headlights. Found myself looking around a little bit too much and not concentrating on getting the ball in the hole.

'Growing up, you always had the putt to win the Masters. On the putting green; this putt's to win the Masters. To actually be here is awesome and to be sitting here on the lead is pretty cool. But it's only Thursday afternoon, so there's a lot of golf to play.' Leishman returns to his house with his family to watch the rest of the day unfold on television. At the throw to every commercial, there's the leader board: M. Leishman −6. Adam Scott is three behind him. Jason Day is −2. Senden is even-par. Day has come out swinging with two bogeys, a double bogey and six birdies.

'I started out a little average,' he says. 'But came home nicely. Made six birdies and really enjoyed playing the back nine. Just got to tighten up a few little soft bogeys out there. If I can do that, then hopefully the momentum will get me going in the right direction.' On the surprise equal leader, Day says: 'Yeah, Leish. That's good. I heard he was under the weather, though. Watch out for the wounded golfer.' Tiger Woods is −2. 'I watch *SportsCenter* on ESPN all the time,' says Leishman. 'It's weird seeing the Masters come up and they're showing me on TV. You see your name on top of the Masters leader board. It felt like I was watching someone else. Obviously you know it's a big deal, it's the Masters, but I'm just a normal bloke.'

·· • ··

Leader Board After Round 1:
−6 Marc Leishman (Australia) 66
−6 Sergio Garcia (Spain) 66
−5 Dustin Johnson (USA) 65
−4 Fred Couples (US) 68

−4 Gonzalo Fernandez-Castano (Spain) 68

−4 Rickie Fowler (USA) 68

−4 Trevor Immelman (South Africa) 68

−4 Matt Kuchar (USA) 68

−4 David Lynn (England) 68

−3 Jim Furyk (USA) 69

−3 Zach Johnson (USA) 69

−3 Adam Scott (Australia) 69

··●··

Furyk!

··●··

And On the Second Day. The Masters as the blank sheet of paper upon which players can write their rags-to-riches tales. The Masters as the recession-proof supplier of vast monetary fortune in reward for hitting a small ball into a hole with a stick. The Masters as the land of milk and honey. The Masters as the place where Jason Day can forge his iden-tity after losing his father too young. Alvin Day found a cut-down 3-wood at the local rubbish tip and thought it might keep his son occupied a while. Day swings it at a tennis ball in the backyard of their property in Queensland. At the age of six, he's hooked. At the age of seven, Alvin is giving him his first look at a proper course. At the age of eleven, his father is diagnosed with stomach cancer. Alvin passes away within months. Day is twelve.

'One of Dad's wishes to Jason was when you make it to Augusta, I want you to sprinkle my ashes, just a few ashes, on that course,' says Day's sister, Kim. 'The worst thing was Jason was twelve at that time. It's a bit hard for a twelve-year-old to take in your dad saying that, because you think your dad is superman and he will never leave you behind. If Dad was around now to see where Jason is today . . . it's hard to even explain what Dad would be like. He would be by his side walking every course with him. Dad would be so proud of who Jason is today. Dad always knew.'

Jason will go off the rails without Alvin. Alcohol and fights will punctuate his teenage years. His mother, Dening, works day and night and takes out a second mortgage to pay for his tuition at the Kooralbyn School in the Gold Coast hinterland. The same school that has already had Adam Scott passing through its corridors. It is Kooralbyn where Day rediscovers golf and meets Col Swatton, the man who will become his coach and caddy. Day hauls his golf bag for a kilometre to practise for three hours before school. His nights are spent reading a book about Tiger Woods. Rather than thinking Woods' feats can never be matched, Day dreams of all the ways he can take Woods down.

Aspirations need to be built on a considerable degree of realism, of course, and Day really does have the stuff. He wins the world junior championship. He turns professional at nineteen. TaylorMade hands him a sizeable contract when he hits irons at their testing factory at Carlsbad, California, with the club head speed most pros only obtain with their drivers. He pays off his mother's debts, spending the change on a Cadillac Escalade. *Golf* magazine runs an article headlined: Meet the World No. 1. 'Oh, man,' Day says of Woods. 'Everyone is working toward something. I'm trying to work toward taking that No. 1 spot from him.' He becomes the youngest Australian to win on the US PGA Tour when he takes out the 2010 Byron Nelson Championship.

Returning to Australia, he proclaims the mission to overtake Woods. What's wrong with ambition? And telling the truth? He is rubbished as a smart alec. 'The whole Tiger Woods thing was a little bit taken out of context,' says Swatton. 'I was there and I know what he said. They asked him what he wanted to do. Basically the way it was put across was that he wanted to be the No. 1 player in the world. At that point Tiger Woods happened to be the No. 1 player in the world. In order for him to be the No. 1, he had to beat Tiger Woods. It could have been anyone. Woods wasn't the main part of it. Trying to be No. 1 was the main thing. I would not say he is a cocky guy but he is definitely confident in his ability. He's confident in what he can achieve on the golf course. He's just always been a very confident young man.

'I don't know whether it comes necessarily from his mum or his dad, but Dening is that way. Jason backs it up with hard work and results. I would never say he is arrogant. He is just confident about what he can do. If you don't believe you can ultimately be the No. 1 player in the world, then what are you on the PGA Tour for? To use one of the great quotes from *Talladega Nights*—if you're not first, you're last. Jason is dead right. If you tee it up every week on the PGA Tour and your goal is not to win, or if your goal is not at the end of your career or at some point in your career to have been the No. 1 player in the world, then what are you playing for? Top 70, top 50, top 125?

'I think Jason truly believes he can be the No. 1 player in the world and he is prepared to work really hard to get it. Occasionally he loses focus and priorities change and he might need a little push or poke in the right direction. But I have said from day one that Jason Day's greatest attribute is his ability to listen and to learn and to want to develop. That's what sets him apart and that is what has made him successful so far. We have an understanding that if he slacks off a little bit, I have the okay to give him a little push or a prod. And vice versa—if I slack off he has the push and the prod. It's an understanding that if he is to be the No. 1 player in the world at some point in his career, he needs to do what he needs to do. If he needs to be reminded of that, then he needs to be reminded of it. That goes with the territory.'

·· ● ··

Scott On Day Two. He bogeys the third when his approach is short, when his chip clunks off the back of the green and when he needs two putts to find the cup. Too loose. He bogeys the fourth with the kind of wild tee shot that bedevilled him in 2009. Another iron is pulled so far wide it would have missed the green by close to 100 metres without the intervention of a pine. It's basically a duck hook with an iron, thudding into the top of the tree and dropping fortuitously near enough to the green. Terrific chip, but he misses the par putt. The bogey opportunity is even longer. The putter! The petard. He's going backwards. And then he bogeys the fifth, too, hurtling towards an 80 if he keeps this up. A birdie on 7 to soothe the soul. He starts finding fairways and greens as though we're in a video game. Sensible pars on the way home are complemented by birdies on 14, where another demanding pin has been cut on what looks like the crest of an unbroken wave, and 18. Nothing puts a spring in the step like a birdie on 18. Nothing gets you up in the morning with more vigour. Scott escapes with a regulation 72.

'I mean, even-par in these conditions is a good score,' he says. 'Even-par or better. No one's doing a lot out there. Tough conditions today. Everything was thrown at us and the pins are really tough. It's easy to make mistakes. I didn't make too many and I managed to hit a few good ones to make birdie. You have to scramble very, very well not to drop shots around here. The wind was swirling and then gusty at times and then moving twenty, 30, 40 degrees quickly from hole to hole. It's really hard to judge shots and pick clubs and pick the lines to hit it on. I haven't really looked at what's leading at the moment, but I've just got to stay in touch. I'm sure there's some players that must be bunched. So it's going to be an interesting weekend and if there's any wind at all, it's going to play tough. I would love to play the par fives a little better, but some days you just can't force the issue. Hopefully I'll have plenty of chances to attack on the weekend.'

Scott is in the top ten. Just. For now, it will do.

•• ● ••

Leishman On Day Two. He makes three pars to break the ice and then the argument begins. A bogey on 4. Another bogey on 6 and he knows what everyone is thinking—Leishman is gone. But he's made of sterner stuff, matching Scott's birdie on 7. Back in business. He birdies 8 to be even for the day. So much revolves around momentum, of riding the favourable moments for all they're worth. The 14th is bogeyed after driving into the pines. Five straight pars calm the turbulence. There's a miracle up-and-down on 16 and all things considered, the final number of 73 is respectable and acceptable. A few bumps and bruises but nothing too serious. One shot off the lead. ESPN *SportsCenter* still has his name on its board.

'The wind was in a different direction and it was stronger than it was yesterday,' he says. 'The two par fives on the back nine, it makes them pretty tough. It was blowing hard at the left on 13 where you have to hit a big hook around the corner. And 15, what's generally reasonably reachable, it's blowing straight in. So probably only the longer hitters can get there today. It made the birdie holes on the back nine not really legitimate birdie holes. They were still birdie chances, but they were pretty tough. To grind it out and only shoot one over around there when I missed a couple of greens in places where you don't want to miss them, left on 16, short on 14; it was good to get out of there relatively unscathed.'

Sounds familiar. Unexpected leaders are prone to avoiding score boards, right? 'I was looking at all of them,' says Leishman. 'But I do that at every tournament, so it's nothing different. I've tried to not do it at a couple of tournaments and it just hasn't worked for me. I like to know where I am, what the situation is, whether I'm ahead, behind, on the cut line, whatever. It's pretty cool to see your name up at the top there with names like Cabrera and Couples. But you know, we're competing against each other, and that's what I've probably learned over the last few years. That those guys are great players but I've got to compete against them and try to beat them. I can't put them on a pedestal. I think I've gotten a little bit better at that, but it's probably going to be hard the next two days, you know, where we are. I've been working hard on the mental part of the game and hopefully it will keep me in good stead for the weekend. Sometimes if you have a low first round, it's hard to back it up. Last time I was here, it was tough on Friday as well, and I let it get away from me and ended up missing the cut. I learned from that. Everything's all right.'

Leishman is asked by an American reporter for the name of the club where he beat his father for the club championship at the age of thirteen. He replies, Warrnambool. What? Warrnambool. What? 'Hopefully I can deal with the weekend pretty well and play good golf,' he says. 'But I know this is different. This is bigger than anything I've probably done before. It's about not getting ahead of myself on the golf course, just conserving energy when I need to conserve energy, not getting frustrated at myself unnecessarily. Just mentally getting better. I do get a little bit angry on the golf course occasionally, and I'm trying to improve that because it does waste a lot of energy.'

Woods has crept towards the top rung of leaders. What does a Marc Leishman think when a Tiger Woods begins to charge? 'Opportunity,' he says. 'Especially when I'm at the top as well. It's a good chance to prove myself. He's the best player in the world at the moment, and obviously I'd have to play good to beat him, but I think it's doable. He'll probably get annoyed now and shoot 62 tomorrow.' All four Australians are in the top eight. 'I saw Jason and Senden are up there,' Leishman says. 'I didn't know Scotty was doing well. Pretty impressive so far. Hopefully it's like that Sunday night. Who knows, maybe one of us can knock it off.'

·· ● ··

Day On Day Two. He will never grind through eighteen consecutive pars. Another cannonball run starts with a bogey on 4. Missing the green to the left, squandering a precious shot, but he replies with an immediate birdie. Of Day's many admirable traits, following a bogey with a birdie is high on the list. Nipping it in the bud. Settling his account before the rot sets in. He takes an iron off the tee on 5. Makes a putt along the ridge, walking a tightrope. And then on the back nine, he pulls the trigger. Birdie on 10! Birdie on 11! A freakish three from the pine straw followed by a snaking downhill putt. No biggie. Bogey on 12. The classic sight of his tee shot hitting the bank and rolling back towards Rae's Creek. Every pro should do it once. Just for kicks. His ball stalls. He does well to get up and down. Fours can become sevens on 12. Birdie on 13! Down. Up! A sensational two on 16, the flared iron landing softly, the wildly hooping putt starting about two metres to the right and semi-circling into the cup. Day does it with giddy ease. With the joy and unpredictability of a kid on a billycart. As though he is simply performing the role he has prepared himself for. He points his putter at the patrons. The debonair golfer. A four up the 18th will give him the overnight lead. He shoots his arrow up the tunnel of a tee. He aims at the bunker, wanting to cut it out to clear land. It stays straight and finds the sand. Day puts his hand to his mouth. Stretches his neck. Scratches his foot. His approach comes up short. There is a putt from off the green. Piece of cake for par.

What a difference a year makes. In the second round of 2012, Day was forced to abandon his round, and the tournament, with an ankle injury. 'Being back on top of the leader board right now is a great honour,' he says. 'I'm really looking forward to getting out there the next two days but I'm also very, very tired. We had almost a six-hour round today. It was very, very difficult. I just have to stay patient, focus on what I'm doing and really not worry about anyone else. If I can go out there and commit to the game plan that me and Col have worked on over the last year, two years, it would be really, really nice to be there come Sunday. There's a lot of pressure on my shoulders being from Australia when no Australian has ever won the event, but I've just got to try to get that out of my mind and plug away. Go out there and really commit.'

Tributes are paid to his bogey-birdie routine on 12 and 13. 'I had the right club on 12,' he says. 'It just—when I was going through impact, I just felt like the club face was slightly open. As soon as I hit it, I knew it was going to stay out there and unfortunately it just didn't have enough power to get over the water. It was actually a very, very good up-and-down for bogey. On 13, I just had to get a 4-wood around the corner. Hit a nice drive there, and a good second shot from 216 yards to just on the right side of the green. It's very difficult when you're playing that hole, once the shade hits the greens, because you can't really see where the slopes are. If it's severe or not so severe—if it goes up and over the slope or not. My putt went past by about eight feet but luckily enough, I holed a good putt coming back down the hill.' He could talk about 13 until dawn.

The fascination of it all. 'The funny thing around here at Augusta is that if you keep it below the trees when it's windy, your ball won't get affected,' he says. 'If you hit it above the trees, that's when it starts getting affected and sometimes it will pull up short or go long. I knew that we had 200 yards to the front edge, and I was pumped. I was amped after the shot that I hit on the tee: a 4-wood, just a nice drawing 4-wood around the corner. I was thinking about hitting 5-iron to the green, but I knew that if I hit 5-iron, it would come out a little higher. I needed to hit a little lower, make sure that the wind wasn't going to affect that second shot.'

Tied for second at your last proper start at Augusta. Now you lead. Something about the joint must resonate. 'It's my favourite tournament,' he says. 'I love this place. Everything I do is about peaking at this event because it's just the best tournament in the world. Coming back here and playing in front of the patrons and just really, like I said before, it's a real honour. Not many people get to say they have had the lead a couple of times at the Masters.' Even fewer can say they have won it.

'I've been trying to follow the corners here, trying to hit to the corners of the course,' he says. 'A lot of people try and work on the draw shot. Obviously you need to hit it both ways here, but I think if you're hitting a nice fade to the corners or even a straight shot to the corners . . . look at 13, for instance. You try to draw it down there, everything slopes to the water. If you're hitting a draw around there and you get a little left, it's going to kick down to the water. So I'm really just trying to play it to the corners and then focus on the second shots. It's really all about the second shots here. If you put yourself in the right position on the greens, you can go out there and think it's the easiest golf course in the world. But there's a lot of tough pins out there, and if you leave yourself above the pins all day, it's the hardest place to play. You need a good short game around here, and the short game was nice today. I putted great, which was good.

'The weather was probably the biggest factor. Trying to stay committed to the shot knowing that— you know, right before I hit my shot on 12, the wind was coming in off the right. And when I hit, when I was right about to hit my shot, it was down off the left. It swirls so much there. Being able to commit to the shot, trusting that the wind is doing whatever you think it is doing, is the biggest key.'

The curse, the hex, the pressure of breaking Australia's drought. 'It's all how you look at it,' he says. 'If you look at it as pressure, you're going to worry about it more. If you look at it as a challenge and an opportunity to be the first and stay positive with it, you know, it only motivates you to play well. So I've just got to really not think about it at all. I really need to stay committed to the plan, stay aggressive to my target, and really aim small and miss small out there. Not worry about anything else but hitting the shot in front of me.'

·· ● ··

Woods posts a 71. For now. He's three off the pace. For now. 'Going back two years ago in the final round, he was five under through nine holes,' says Day. 'So I mean, he can make up the difference in nine holes. I really don't need to worry about him. The moment I start worrying about other players is the moment I start losing focus on what I need to do, and when I do that, I'll start making bogeys. It really is exciting to have the opportunity to win the Masters and I'm very, very happy where I am right now.

'But it's difficult because it's a major. There's so many people watching you hit your shots who are here, so many people watching you hit your shots around the world. So there's obviously a lot of pressure there. I was just trying to breathe as much as I could to keep myself down and level. And I played great. I felt like I played pretty slow, but we couldn't go any faster than the guys in front, and they weren't too far ahead of us. When it means everything to you, you're going to try and do the best you can to play well. And whether that makes you, you know, weigh it up or discuss ten seconds more or twenty seconds more on a shot, you're going to do it. Because at the end of the day, no one is really going to think about how slow you played if you win the tournament. Everyone is going to think about how well you played to win the event.'

··●··

Leader Board After Round 2:
−6 Jason Day (Australia) 70–68
−5 Marc Leishman (Australia) 66–73
−5 Fred Couples (USA) 68–71
−4 Angel Cabrera (Argentina) 71–69
−4 Jim Furyk (USA) 69–71
−4 Brandt Snedeker (USA) 70–70
−3 K.J. Choi (South Korea) 70–71
−3 Jason Dufner (USA) 72–69
−3 David Lynn (England) 68–73
−3 Justin Rose (England) 70–71
−3 Lee Westwood (England) 70–71
−3 Adam Scott (Australia) 69–72

··●··

And On the Third Day. DRAMA. Woods is the elephant in the room at Augusta for the most ridiculous reason of all: the colour of his skin. One of Clifford Roberts' more notorious comments is this: 'As long as I'm alive, golfers will be white and caddies will be black.' It is fair to suggest he never envisioned a black man winning four titles with a white New Zealander on his bag. (Woods' father, Earl, was the son of an African-American who was a Green Beret in Vietnam. He nicknamed his son 'Tiger' after a Vietnamese soldier friend. His mother, Kultida, was the wealthy daughter of a Thai family.) When Woods returned from 45 days in therapy for a sex addiction at the 2010 Masters, Augusta chairman Billy Payne admonished him in headmasterly fashion. Who were we to judge? It would also be fair to assume nothing could stick the knife into Woods more than his own conscience.

Payne delivers a very public condemnation. 'As he now says himself, he forgot in the process to remember that with fame and fortune comes responsibility, not invisibility,' says the chairman. 'It is not simply the degree of his conduct that is so egregious here. It is the fact that he disappointed all of us, and more importantly, our kids and our grandkids. Our hero did not live up to the expectations of the role model we saw for our children. I hope he now realises that every kid he passes on the course wants his swing, but would settle for his smile. We at Augusta hope and pray that our great champion will begin his new life here tomorrow in a positive, hopeful and constructive manner, but this time, with a significant difference from the past. This year, it will not be just for him, but for all of us who believe in second chances. Is there a way forward? I hope yes. I think yes. But certainly his future will never again be measured only by his performance against par, but measured by the sincerity of his efforts to change.' Payne has scoffed at the suggestion Woods' return is bigger than the tournament itself. 'We don't look at things that way,' he says. 'We are very secure in who we are.'

Now Norman and Faldo are calling for Woods to be disqualified for an incorrect drop during yesterday's round. Woods has signed his card without being questioned by officialdom but an interview with ESPN has sparked a chain reaction of criticism, interpretation and judgement. 'I went down to the drop area, that wasn't going to be a good spot, because obviously it's into the grain, it's really grainy there,' Woods says of the incident on the 15th hole. 'And it was a little bit wet. So it was muddy and not a good spot to drop. So I went back to where I played it from, but I went two yards further back and I took, tried to take two yards off the shot of what I felt I hit. And that should land me short of the flag and not have it either hit the flag or skip over the back. I felt that that was going to be the right decision to take off four right there. And I did. It worked out perfectly.' But Woods has breached the rules. He's improved his position. He should have been penalised one stroke but the rules violation is only detected hours after the conclusion of his round thanks to a rules official whose hackles are raised when he hears the interview. Masters suits have reviewed the incident and cleared Woods of any wrongdoing. But the court of public opinion has a different verdict. Woods arrives at Augusta National for day three, on the Saturday morning, to find himself in the crosshairs. Perhaps he will be disqualified for signing an incorrect scorecard. DRAMA.

The chairman of the Masters competition committee, Fred Ridley, instead gives Woods a two-shot penalty. 'In preparation for his fifth shot, the player dropped his ball in close proximity to where he had played his third shot in apparent conformance with Rule 26,' says Ridley. 'After being prompted by a television viewer, the Rules Committee reviewed a video of the shot while he was playing the 18th hole. At that moment and based on that evidence, the committee determined he had complied with the Rules. The subsequent information provided by the player's interview after he had completed play warranted further review and discussion with him this morning. The penalty of disqualification was waived by the committee under Rule 33 as the committee had previously reviewed the information and made its initial determination prior to the finish of the player's round. Based on his forthright answers to the questions I had, I told Tiger, in light of that information that he had in fact violated the rules and will be penalised. Because we had initially made the determination the previous day, having viewed his round from TV, we elected to make the decision, under Rule 33–7, to give him a two-shot penalty. This is about integrity, if it had been "John Smith", he would have been given the same ruling.'

All the John Smiths sincerely doubt it. Norman leads the outpourings of displeasure. 'It is all about the player and the integrity of the game,' he tweets. 'Woods violated the rules as he played. [Being No. 1] carries a greater burden. WD for the game.' Wayne Grady agrees: 'Absolute rubbish. It's not a trial by video situation. Tiger came into a press conference to say he intentionally dropped the ball, he admitted to doing that in his post-round press conference. Absolutely [he should be disqualified].'

Faldo deposits his two bobs' worth: 'He still has time, if he is smart and if he understands we have got to uphold the rules of this game, the gentlemanly conduct and the integrity of our game. We are custodians of it and we carry that forward. All those guys who have called their playing partners over and said "I took the club back and it has rolled". They have moved a quarter of an inch, what difference does it make? But you say "Sorry mate, add a shot". This is a very historic moment in our game and Tiger could come out of it with good brownie points and say "No, you are right". He took advantage and he knows he took advantage.'

Woods is given a triple-bogey eight on the 15th. His 71 is amended to a 73. Instead of being tied for fourth with Day and Leishman at five under, he's equal seventh with South African Tim Clark at three under. Sticks and stones: Woods is in the top ten. And he's still in the tournament. These are his only concerns.

·· ● ··

Day three is moving day. The mad scramble. The jockeying for positions. Every hole at Augusta is capable of telling a story. Every hole has a name. In order of appearance: Tea Olive, Pink Dogwood, Flowering Peach, Flowering Crab Apple, Magnolia, Juniper, Pampas, Yellow Jasmine, Carolina Cherry, Camellia, White Dogwood, Golden Bell, Azalea, Chinese Fir, Firethorn, Redbud, Nandina, Holly. Eighteen characters in the play.

·· • ··

Moving Day for Scott. Par, par, birdie. Yes. Moving in the right direction. He conducts himself in the appropriate manner. There's an air of authority. Six pars to get the ball rolling. Not getting into it. More importantly, he is not getting out of it. The clock is ticking down, however, to when affirmative action will be required. A bogey on 10. Stay calm. You know how to do this. Adam Scott needs to be sure to birdie 13. He birdies 13. He needs to be sure to birdie 15. He birdies 15. An old hand by now. Go on, birdie 17. He birdies 17.

A round of 69 after five hours of the Titleist being on a piece of string. A round when a bazooka of a drive has reduced the 350-yard second hole to pitch and putt with your mates on a Friday night. A round when he has exuded such effortless control that Steve Williams has almost appeared downright casual. Almost. A round where his drives down the par fives on the back nine have carried enough club head speed to snap his shafts in half. A round where an eagle putt can miss by one inch but because the glass is half full, there's only a one-inch putt for birdie and that will do nicely. A round where he has that glazed in-contention look: his entire existence revolves around the next shot. A round where he has a taste of the luck so often required to win the Masters: his approach to the 11th green has landed short and started drawing back towards the water, only to stop on the embankment. He flicks his chip too long and swipes the grass in frustration. It is one thing to receive favour. You have to make the most of it. But he curls in the putt. A four instead of a six. He walks off with a sense of purpose. There might even be an air of destiny. Here's a round that includes a birdie on 17 when he sculpts a putt of immaculate line and length when disaster has otherwise beckoned.

'Look, today was a great day,' he says. 'Even with no wind, the course was tricky. The greens were firming out and getting faster. Had to be careful where you attacked. I just kind of figured it out as I went around. By about the fourth hole I had an understanding of how the greens were playing for the day, and what that would mean for certain pin positions as we made our way around the course. I played fairly cautiously, and that was kind of a blessing in disguise. I drove it well, but I had a couple of steps in the rough and had to be cautious coming out of there. That wasn't a bad way to play. It worked out for me. Even made a couple of putts.'

· · ● · ·

Moving Day for Day. Twelve straight pars! Lost his mind! When you think you know someone. Day is playing with Fred Couples. His first two rounds have comprised one double bogey, four bogeys, twelve birdies, eighteen pars and an eagle. His scorecards resemble games of noughts and crosses. Now he goes mainstream? He sits still and he waits. He has to chip sideways from the trees on the par-five fifth but regardless, another metronomic par. A birdie on 13. His drive has bounced off a tree and nestled in the light rough. He steals his birdie and grins from ear to ear. There is something of the cheeky bugger in Jason Day. Something wholly unique and independent.

Right when he is about to close down a polished round that has him tied for the lead with Angel Cabrera and Brandt Snedeker, he makes bogey from the middle of the 17th fairway. Come on, concentrate. Putting across the weird shadows of his own legs, the putt skids out of control. He grabs the collar of his shirt and pulls it across his mouth. Swear jar. A birdie on 18 will make up for it but he stumbles to another bogey from prime position. From what Newton calls the mayor's office. The birdie putt slides eight feet past. And he misses the putt for par. He's taken sixteen steps forward and two backwards. A bogey-bogey finish in the first onslaught of nerves.

'I was patient enough out there, unfortunately three-putted 17 and 18, but I'm not too disappointed,' he says. 'Obviously I would love to have the lead, but I'm only a couple back.'

Couples fears he contributed to Day's blunder on 17 by chopping around for a quadruple bogey while Day was growing stale on the green. 'I feel bad for Jason because he was—he waited for me forever on the 17th and then I finally thought to myself, I'm not going to make him wait, and I said, why don't you go. And then he hit and he three-putted. His three-putt on 18 was all on his own, but 17 I felt like I was killing him there. It took me forever to figure out how to make a seven.'

Replies Day: 'No, no, no. I three-putted but I wasn't really paying attention to what he was doing. When I'm out there I've got to pay attention to what I'm doing. Freddie is such a nice guy and he meant well by saying that, but he's not hitting my putts for me.'

·· ● ··

Moving Day for Leishman. He plays with the broad-shouldered Cabrera and when he birdies the second from a trap he's zooming along the Great Ocean Road at breakneck speed. But then comes a bogey on 4 and his first bad swing on the fifth: the old chestnut of abandoning the follow-through because it looks and feels so ugly. He's standing in his third bunker from four holes. No!

A birdie on 7 offers relief. Then he goes birdie-birdie as though he's skipping through Amen Corner on tournament's eve. He's in a precarious position for two on the par-five eighth. Needs to hit it about 20 metres in the air to travel the ten metres to the pin and land softly. It carries great risk.

It must be hit with a full swing. If impact is imperfect, the ball could land in the Savannah. Impact is perfect! Birdie. Leishman finds the water on 11, but sinks a monstrous putt for bogey. That'll do. Run. A towering birdie on 13. A missed tiddler on 14. The patrons go 'Ugh' as if they have been punched in the stomach. Leishman keeps throwing punches. Birdie on 16 when the pond is glistening. He stiffs it and the place goes nuts. Where's he from? Warrnambool. Where? Warrnambool. Bogey on 17.

Adding up his card will take a while: there are red numbers, black numbers, circles, squares: after all that, he signs for an even-par 72. Five birdies, five bogeys. Three days after the stunner of his first round, with his fifteen-month-old son making head nor tail of it all, Leishman has hung tough enough to be in the hunt for Sunday. Bravo.

•• • ••

Leader Board After Round 3:
−7 Angel Cabrera (Argentina) 71−69−69
−7 Brandt Snedeker (USA) 70−70−69
−6 Adam Scott (Australia) 69−72−69
−5 Jason Day (Australia) 70−68−73
−5 Marc Leishman (Australia) 66−73−72

–4 Matt Kuchar (USA) 68–75–69

–3 Tim Clark (South Africa) 70–67–76

–3 Tiger Woods (USA) 70–73–70

–2 Rickie Fowler (USA) 68–76–70

–2 Jim Furyk (USA) 69–71–74

–2 Bernhard Langer (Germany) 71–71–72

–2 Steve Stricker (USA) 73–70–71

–2 Lee Westwood (England) 70–71–73

6

THE BACK NINE ON A SUNDAY

'Our overall aim at the Augusta National has been to provide a golf course of considerable natural beauty, enjoyable for the average golfer and at the same time testing for the expert player trying to better par. We want to make bogeys easy if frankly sought, pars readily obtainable by standard good play, and birdies, except on par fives, dearly bought.'
Bobby Jones

The Green Jacket is All. 'Always loved the place,' says Nicklaus. 'Had that love affair with the thing. When I first came here in '59, Bob Jones put a note in my locker. He invited my father and me down to his cabin, and we went down every year. That same note was in my locker every year. It actually was more talk about golf than anything . . . a lot of philosophy for life. How he led his life and what he believed in and why he stayed an amateur and why he played amateur golf and some of the issues of why he quit and stopped playing. He knew this young kid had a chance to be a pretty good player, and he wanted to impart as much wisdom to him as he could. And it was just his way of saying, hey, I'm on your side, I want to see you do well and I want to help you wherever I can.

'Then coming here in '63, I was the US Open champion and I felt like I had really prepared and wanted to play. I had hurt my hip early in the year, and I had had 25 injections in my hip over a ten-week period, which is probably why I've had my hip replaced. But what it forced me to do was learn how to play right-to-left because I couldn't hit it in my hip. I couldn't play left-to-right. And so it was actually very fortuitous for me here because I was able to learn how to play around my left side and learn how to hook the ball. And so when I got here, I was happy with what I was doing. I didn't play very well the first round. I shot 74.

'I came back with 66 the second round. And then we had the rain day. It just poured and everybody thought—in those days when they washed out a round, they washed out the whole round. They didn't start back at the same place. So I remember the 13th fairway, we had total 100 per cent casual water and there was no place to drop it, and they said tough, play it. So we played it out of the water. Anyway, nobody thought we would finish the round. We finished, we got to the 18th green and that's when I looked at the leader board. I'm colourblind, and I looked at the leader board and I saw these several ones on the board. And I looked at my caddie, Willie Peterson, and I said, "Willie, how many of those ones are red?" And he said, "Just you, Boss." And that's when I found out I was leading the tournament. I finished it off the next day. I don't even remember what I shot the last two rounds, but I won the tournament.

'Arnold put a green jacket on me, and it was a size 46 long. I could have used it for an overcoat. I was a 43 regular. But the story goes on beyond that. Obviously I was excited about winning the Masters, but the next year I came back and they didn't have a coat for me. They said, here, use this one. It was Tom Dewey's coat. The former governor of New York—Tom Dewey was a 43 regular. The coat fit me perfect, and I wore that for about ten years. They just kept putting Tom Dewey's coat on me every time I won the Masters. It got around to 1998 and we were doing the fountain for Clifford Roberts, and I told Jack Stephens the story about never being given a green jacket: I've won six times and nobody has ever given me one. And he said, "What?" I said, "No, I've never been presented a green jacket. Jack, I have no problem with that. But I told him, I'm the only guy that's ever won this tournament and never got one." I went home that weekend, came back, and there was a note in the locker: you will go to the pro shop and get your green jacket. So now I have a green jacket. Same one.'

Another is up for grabs.

••●••

Perhaps It Will Be Cabrera. 'Angel has no fear,' says his coach, Charlie Epps. 'I know his state of mind. There are nerves, but he has no actual fear. He's matured so much in his golf. He's in charge. He's his own man because he's been on his own since he was two years old.' Say what? 'His mum and dad, they gave him away to his grandmother. So he grew up without a mum and dad. He grew up on the streets of a city called Cordoba, fighting for himself. Catch as catch can. That is just amazing to me. The day he won the US Open in 2007, walking up the 18th hole that Sunday afternoon, I figured he had walked 45,000 miles in his life. From walking back and forth to the golf course at Cordoba, from walking around the course caddying, from not getting a car until he was 23 and then walking as a professional. The journey has been a long, long, winding road for him. He has done himself proud. He's just been a hard-working kid with an extreme amount of talent, but a lot of desire. He's taking steps towards the Hall of Fame—it's a pretty good story.'

Epps was in the room in San Francisco when Norman told Cabrera he was to be lumbered with Scott at the Presidents Cup. 'It was very evident that Adam was struggling,' says Epps. 'But he was trying. They had a great match together. On the second hole, Adam couldn't even hit the green with a 7-iron, but he really was trying. His mental game was off. That's what can happen to top athletes. They don't lose their talent. They just lose their way for a while. Mentally they get a little upside down. Maybe it was because he knew how he was playing coming in. It really wasn't said that much, it was just kind of inferred. I was there with Angel because I was his coach and translator. All those guys love Adam, he is the nicest guy on tour, and he works hard. It's the guys who persevere and hang in there during the tough times who are going to survive. That's one thing about Australians, they keep persevering. I would say Angel has great feelings about Adam because they're both real nice people. They don't go out and drink beer together, it's a professional relationship, but they respect each other's games and persona. Angel was thrown into that situation of playing with Adam at the Presidents Cup and sure, everybody was surprised. But Angel said, "Let's go," and now they're in this position at the Masters.'

Memories of 2009, and now.

'Angel's mood was outstanding,' Epps says. 'So nice and loose. His attitude all week was to shoot under par every day. He woke up on the Sunday this year and it was a great day, the kind of day it was for him when he won it. He'll always handle the situation very well. He's very calm. We're staying about five miles from the course and the night before, we just sat around the barbie and had a little meat. A couple of guys came over and we told some stories. We acted like men around a barbie.

'The next morning, I got up and went to Starbucks, getting the coffees and taking them back to the house. We had toast and hung around, Angel answered a few phone calls, people were calling him. We got to the course and went through our routine. We started off with some putting drills. Then he went to the range and went through his bag. He hits six to eight balls with every club. Then we go over to the chipping and putting green. He does some sand play. I'm always monitoring the clock so we're not rushed. Then we go to the caddie area and have a little bite to eat, nothing fancy. Back over to the putting green and with about ten minutes to go, he hits about five minutes of putts from 30 feet. He walks to the tee like he's walking into a practice round.'

A little bite to eat? When Cabrera is in charge of the menu for the Champions Dinner in 2010, he organises an Argentine-style grilled meat called morcilla, or blood sausage. Told of the menu, Jack Nicklaus squirms: 'I hope he enjoys it.'

·· ● ··

Perhaps It Will Be Day. 'Now's a good opportunity to go out there and win my first major,' he says. 'Masters Sunday is nerve-racking so patience is going to be the key. There's going to be a lot of ups and downs. I just have to get off to a good start and hang around. That's pretty much what I learned two years ago. I just hung around and I was right in it at the end. It's going to be a waiting game again, trying to make as many pars and as many birdies as I can. If it happens for me, that's great. If it doesn't, I'll keep plugging away.

'I know people expect me to play well in majors. I know they expect me to win and because of that, it's hard not to put pressure on myself. I'll be playing practice rounds and people will yell out, go get 'em this week! I have money on you! All these things add up and you start to feel a bit of a weight on your shoulders. It's why I don't read articles about myself anymore. People can write some mean, mean stuff on the internet. The tough guy behind the computer because they don't have to face you. It's unfortunate, but I had to stop reading all of it, whether it's good, bad or indifferent.'

Day's first taste of public backlash has followed his rookie claim that he wants to be world No. 1. 'When I first came out and said that, Tiger was dominating,' he says. 'I got a lot of flack for it. But like I've always said, you can't blame a guy for trying to be the best at his profession. I'm sure people back home understand my goal has always been to be No. 1. But people write some mean stuff about that, too. Then you bring in people who start writing things about my wife. My wife at the Masters one year, she blew up. She went nuts in the Twitter world. I just try to keep things private now because I've been hurt a few times.'

He possesses a bulging property portfolio and a selection of prized automobiles. He's been lauded and rubbished: labelled traitorous for not playing enough Australian tournaments while simultaneously nominated as his country's next sporting mega-star. Already he leads an extraordinary existence.

'It's very easy to get a big head in sport if you're good at your profession,' he says. 'It's easy to get loud and think you're the man. Especially over here in America, you have a lot of people coming up to you and giving you so much love. That's a good thing but you can go two ways with that. I want to be pretty humble. Over the last few years I've realised that certain things I say can come across big-headed. It's like teaching a little kid to say thank you and please. I have a good support team around me that give me a lot of crap. If I say something stupid, they let me know. I've had a lot of good life experiences that can be distractions, but I'm glad to be getting all of this out of the way early.

'It's funny how far I have come from losing Dad and growing up on a farm. A bunch of things I wouldn't wish on another kid, but all those things in the past have just added to the strength and the willpower to try to improve. I've worked really, really hard to get here. I'm enjoying the stuff that I feel like I deserve because I worked so hard for it. I didn't go out and party with my friends. When I was in high school I didn't have much of a social life. All I did was eat, drink and sleep golf. It's good to see it's paying off. Obviously I can't stop now. There are certain life goals I want to get to—a journey can start but I know you have to remind yourself to enjoy yourself along the way.

'The moment I got some money, I paid Mum's house off. I wanted her to stress less about having mortgage payments and things. When I went and paid it off, straight away she went out and bought something else. She put herself straight back into the mortgage payments. That's the way Mum is.

She's a very hard worker, and I work hard like she does. I'm very, very happy she is still around and can enjoy it. Hopefully one day she can move to America and be closer to me.'

Day has become a father to a one-year-old son, Dash. 'Even now, I can see myself when I'm retired,' he says. 'I see myself having a foundation. I see myself helping people that need to be helped. I didn't come from a silver spoon. I came from a pretty hard upbringing. As long as I can give to others and let them experience certain things I didn't experience, I'm going to be very happy with that. My main goal in life is to be the best I can be. I see myself as a father and a good husband to Ellie. With all the fame and fortune you can possibly have in this game of golf, to be one of the nicest guys you can come across, that's what I want to be. I want to be a good person and respected, and I'm just really looking forward to the next 30 years of my life. I want to have fun being me.

'I want to be No. 1 in the world, and then I'm not going to play the senior tour. I want to play for somewhere between fifteen and twenty years and accomplish a lot of goals. I want to win as many majors as I can and maintain the No. 1 spot for as long as I can. I want to be a golfer who is a contender each and every week. If you can win two or three times a year, you will have a great career. I would like to be one of those guys and get into the Hall of Fame. I'm trying to set myself up so that I can have an easy life later on. Right now I'm just trying to take care of business. I don't like to have debt. I don't like having mortgage payments. I'm trying to make the right decisions now.'

He acknowledges the lunacy in targetting the No. 1 ranking as a teen. 'I was a good young player and my game was heading in the right direction,' he says. 'Being sixteen, seventeen at the time, I'd only been to the States a couple of times. I barely got out of Australia but then I started to explore the world, different players, and work out how good they were compared to me. Col and I sat down and talked about the No. 1 thing. We had a plan to turn professional young. We stuck with that plan. I asked him, "Can I get to No. 1 in the world?" He said yeah, of course. We both said it's going to take a lot of hard work and dedication because it's not easy to get to that level. We had a plan and obviously we're still trying to get there right now. I'm not too far away but I still have to play a lot of good golf to get to No. 1. It's the same old story. It's a slow process.

'When I first came out on the PGA Tour, I thought it was going to be easy. Unfortunately, I went backwards. So I re-dedicated myself. I realised I needed to work harder. Now I've had the best two years of my career because I'm doing the little things right. It's about dedication and sacrifice. They're pretty much the two words that stick out. They're what make the difference. The plan was to be No. 1 at the age of 23 and while we didn't get that right, we're still having a seriously good run at it. The funniest thing is that at fifteen or sixteen, it was a very long-term goal for me. To be talking about getting to No. 1 in the world at sixteen, in the back of your head you're subconsciously thinking, "Do you really think you can get there?" There have been doubts but it's always been the goal and I can't stop until I get there.'

·· ● ··

Perhaps It Will Be Scott. 'It's going to be an amazing Sunday again at the Masters,' he says. 'A couple of years ago here, I felt like I did everything I could. It wasn't enough. That's how it goes. It's going to take a great round tomorrow because there are so many great players right there. I know someone else is going to play well, so I need a career round. That's what these big events do for someone. It's a career round that makes them a champion. You just kind of have to roll with it a little bit on the course and see what it offers up and pick your spots where you can actually be a little bit aggressive, because you're going to have to make some birdies to be in the hunt. You can't just sit back and play defensive. We're all playing well so you can't just sit around and wait for it to happen. You have to pick your moments and that's what will be the difference between the guy who wins and the guys who don't.

'We've got another great chance to win one for Australia. A couple of us had a look at it a couple years ago, and three of us are right there knocking on the door again tomorrow. It's hard to say exactly what it would mean. Aussies are proud sporting people and we'd love to put another notch in our belt. It's one thing that all of us would like to do tomorrow. But I'd rather not sit here and wonder so much. I'd rather do that if I win tomorrow.'

In Steve Williams he trusts: 'It's great to know I've got a rock on the bag next to me. He's solid. I know he has a level of comfort around this place and he's realising that I've developed a level of comfort here, too. We're not treading on each other's toes. More and more, we are on the same wavelength. That's what you're looking for in this kind of relationship. His experience might count for a lot.'

And in himself he trusts. 'I just didn't know how to play the majors in years past,' he says. 'I just didn't play smart enough or well enough, for that matter. My confidence was too easily affected by a poor shot, or a poor hole, and I was a bit too fragile. But there's a lot more to it. Part of the preparation and the way you get ready protects you from being fragile. It's not easier, none of this is easy, but it feels a little easier than when it wasn't coming at all.'

The turning point? 'Identifying a few things at the start of 2011 and changing my schedule,' he says. 'Being a bit different and doing it the way I believed was best, and the way the people around me felt was best, and not necessarily doing what everyone else does. Just doing things the way that worked for me. It can be hard to do when you're in a routine out there on the tour, but I had to step out of that to play a lot less tournaments. I've seen the results and a bit of a balance. I've had less chances to win tournaments, but more chances to win majors. I wanted my focus to be on the majors, so I'm achieving what I wanted to achieve.'

All so calm and balanced. Ever had a tantrum? 'Sure he has,' says Phil. 'As a kid, like every kid when it gets on top of them. I can remember him throwing a couple of clubs. I can certainly remember chatting with him once after he had thrown one, giving him the standard chat that every kid gets from someone in their group at the club, or the pro. If you do that again, you won't be playing sort of thing. This was early days. I'm thinking he was thirteen. Certainly in his later junior days I don't recall it at all. As you can imagine, over those years and all those rounds, he will have been angry—but he masks it pretty well. I just think he has that genetic make-up. His mum is the same. Pam is very serene. They're not interested in conflict. Some people like a spat— Adam and Pam are the opposite. They never do things to create an argument.'

So he doesn't have his old man's genes? 'He's certainly got the competitive thing from me,' says Phil. 'I've always been competitive in sport.' Speaking of perfection: the swing. It really is perfect, agreed? 'Whether we should use the word perfect or not— it's subjective,' says Phil. 'But Adam was just a dream to teach. You would say to him you need to be in this position, show him, and he would get there straight away. He was so easy to coach and then it was pretty easy to keep him on track because when you showed him something and explained it properly to him, he could just do it. You didn't have to spend a month hitting balls to get to a new position.'

The Tiger clone. 'Certainly not,' protests Phil. 'We used to get accused of Adam having Tiger's swing but the truth of all that is really simple: I coached Adam until he was twenty and I had never seen Tiger Woods swing a golf club. That throws that out the window. The Butch Harmon thing— and Butch has said this a lot to me—is that he didn't base anything with Adam on what Tiger was doing. Adam already had the golf swing he has now. What they worked on, certainly in the first couple of years when Adam was with Butch, were things like width on the downswing, which was very similar to what he was working on with Tiger.

'But at that point in their careers, and both of their body shapes have changed dramatically since, they were both six-foot guys with a similar physique, a modern golf swing, not the old-fashioned golf swing. To put the right picture in your mind and relate it to something you hear all the time, for years you would have heard Tiger say, "I got stuck behind myself". That's the opposite of having width in the downswing. And because they move their bodies so quickly to start the downswing, if the club came down narrow, they wouldn't have time to release it. So they were always working on trying to be wide to start down. Butch worked on that with Adam, and he was working on it with Tiger, so it kind of looked like a mimic.

'But Butch has said to me if you looked at Adam before he ever worked on him—I mean, I can still remember sitting in Butch's indoor bay the first time Adam went to see him hit some balls, and Butch said to me: "Holy shit, it's like watching Tiger three years ago." I had never seen Tiger so it wasn't possible for us to mimic his action. By then I knew who Tiger was, of course, but none of that was relevant. It was more a fluke of very similar body shapes, and what you were doing with the golf swing at that time. You were working on this width and clearance. It just ended up looking similar.'

Was the swing based on your own? 'Certainly not mine,' he grins. 'More moving parts than a Swiss watch. My theory on golf is that simple is always best. Simple golf swings work, so the less going on the better.' Ever sit back and admire your handiwork? 'Yeah I did. By his late teens he just swung it and hit it awfully good. I used to think, "How good is that". I used to watch him hit shots and think, "That is proper golf, you have to be really good to hit that shot". I've watched millions of good players, and I think the same thing with only some of the players on tour: God, that is special. Rory McIlroy is one of them. Some of the others don't have that bit extra. There's a different sound when they hit it, and a different trajectory and shape. I admire those guys just as much in some ways because I think, "The guy hasn't got much, but he is still one of the best players in the world". You can just see the differences.

'There's maybe half a dozen guys on tour at a different level in how they hit the ball. The square-up in golf is always about the short-game stuff because potentially your grandmother can be the best chipper and putter in the world. It doesn't require great physique or strength. So there's a lot of guys who have worked that out. Let's pick a famous guy. Jim Furyk. Forgetting it even looks quirky, he can't overpower a course. He can't hit freakish shots. He's just awfully good because he plays to his strengths. To a lesser degree, an Aussie guy like Nick O'Hern. Watch him hit it and you think, "He's no better than me". But he's awfully good at what he does.'

Phil denies offence at the Woods comparisons. 'That's not the word I would use at all because to some degree, you would say there is a level of being flattered,' he says. 'Tiger is the best player, or the second best player, that's ever lived. It's not a bad thing to be compared to him. But I suppose as time went on we got a bit sick of it because it was generally promoted by people that you would think would know better. In fact they weren't involved at all and therefore didn't know anything. Certainly from my point of view, I would say I was never offended—that would be too strong a word. But I thought it was ignorant. How could you make that comment when you didn't know. I get it if you say Adam's swing looks like Tiger's. But I don't get it if you say he modelled it on Tiger. How do you know that? You weren't there.

'Probably surprisingly, you would find Ad and Tiger didn't even practise and play together a lot, anyway. Not as much as you would think.

Realistically, when Adam was there, Tiger wasn't and vice versa. In all the years with Butch, Adam might have played with Tiger only ten or fifteen times. The first time, Tiger touched him up a bit. I think they played for $100. Might have been $100 a hole. Tiger put the foot down. That's him. He figures, "I will show you right now that you're not going to beat me, son." If you think any top athlete is competitive, which they all are, Woods is super competitive.

'Adam came away from that knowing he had work to do. He thought it a lot of times in his early years on tour. I can remember him playing with Jose Maria Olazabal at a tournament in England. Adam did well. I think he ran fifth or something as a kid. But he came off the course saying boy, do I have some work to do on my short game. You want to watch this Jose Maria hit it. He's a genius. There was a lot of that in those early years. Playing with Ernie and saying, how good was that? Just realising how good those guys really are. I am sure that happens to all of them and then the trick or the luck—or the combinations thereof—makes you lift your standard to get there yourself. Adam has always thought he could do it. He's always been the glass-full type. He's a lot more determined than people give him credit for.'

·· ● ··

Perhaps It Will Be Leishman. His father contemplates their surroundings. 'To watch your son play here is pretty amazing,' he says. 'I laid bricks for 35 years. I was always a golfer, and then I started working with the pro at our local course, helping with the golf and sending fields off just to get out of laying bricks. I'm a scratch marker and used to play a lot. I was captain of the golf club for a few years when Marc was a little fella. He used to tag along and it just went from there. He won his first club champion-ship when he was thirteen. That was a really good day. I was playing in the same group as him: we have four rounds of stroke play like a normal golf tournament. I played with him in the last round because we were pretty close in the championship. He got me. Well, he got everyone. It was pretty amazing. When you look back at it now, compared to the Masters, it's pretty insignificant but it wasn't at the time.

'We used to watch the Masters together. I'd be watching it before I went to work. Marc would get up and watch it with me before he went to school. We always wanted an Aussie to win it. A lot of the guys at the golf club say to me, you're living the dream a bit now, going over there and watching your son play on the American PGA Tour. I say I am, but the Masters experience is at another level again. Like Marc says, it's only another tournament. That's how he looks at it, just trying to keep level-headed. But when you get over here, it's actually not. They treat it a little differently.'

Being here is no fluke. The financial sacrifices have been immense. 'I always thought he'd be a good golfer,' says Paul. 'He was probably about four years old when I gave him a club to muck around with. Obviously dad likes to get his son into it. He loved his football and cricket. He still loves his cricket, but golf was always number one. It was always going to be the one he would go on with. We played a lot together when he was growing up.

'We have a Thursday afternoon comp in Warrnambool. Some days I'd be laying bricks and when I got home from work, Marc would have knocked off school at lunchtime and played golf with the boys all afternoon for money. This would have been when he was about sixteen. He would pull a sickie from school. These mates of mine, who played for a little bit of money, they would ring me and say, is it all right if Marc plays? I would say I cannot afford to have him playing for money. They would say, we'll back him. I'd knock off work of a Thursday evening, buggered, and grab a beer out of the fridge. He would come home with $90 in his pocket. I've worked all day to get $100. He wouldn't give it away, don't worry about that. Marc is still the same—he won't eat at extravagant restaurants or stay in extravagant hotels. He is still down to earth. He has good roots.

'Money was hard early. When he started it was hard for us to get money and I think he's remembered that. He was showing potential and we thought if you can't do it for your kids, what can you do? We'll give it a crack here. If it works, it works. If it doesn't work, you haven't really lost anything. It cost a lot of money. We have a daughter, and she missed out in those early days, but Marc looks after her now. He appreciates what happened and what she didn't get because it was given to him.

'I have a good mate who has a car dealership. I remember I bought a Ford Fairlane back in about 1998, or something like that. He said you're going to wear this car out on the kid, aren't you? We did. We were sometimes in Melbourne twice a week from Warrnambool, which is a three-and-a-half-hour drive. Once he got into the junior state teams, they would have training and meetings in Melbourne. They said if you want him to be in these things, you have to be there. Sometimes it was an eight-hour round trip for us. It cost us a lot of money and a lot of time. People in Melbourne would travel half an hour each way and it was a hassle for them. But they're the sacrifices you make.

'He went in a natural progression. Every time he stepped up the standard of tournament, he would win again. When he got to the senior state level and he was winning tournaments there, I was thinking there could be a future here. Obviously my wife and I—she is a nurse and I was a bricklayer—we just worked virtually our whole life to keep him going. Golf can be an expensive sport when they're travelling all around Australia. He was lucky enough to get in the Institute of Sport. They funded a lot of his overseas trips, which was a godsend for us because money was tight. He won everything he could as an amateur. He got his Australian Tour card and ended up in Korea for twelve months because he wanted to get a bank. The big picture was that he always wanted to try America. Korea was tough, it was really tough for him. He played well over there but it was obviously very different. The people were different, the language barrier made it harder. But he did what he wanted to do. He got a bank and that's when he went to America. He would go in the Monday qualifying for the Nationwide Tour. Nothing was handed to him.'

From the back blocks of Monday qualifying for low-level American tours to being within reach of the Masters. 'The greens are getting faster and firmer,' Leishman says. 'I've heard that's what Augusta is all about. I'm looking forward to getting out there on a Sunday and seeing it for myself. It's different on the weekend. The Saturday felt different to the Thursday and Friday. The fans have been a little bit more vocal. It's a lot of fun—*a lot of fun*—and I keep learning more about the course with all the rounds I'm getting under my belt. I'm hitting the ball well. Just got to hole the putts. I'm well and truly in it but I need a low one and who knows, maybe we can take that Australian curse off. Three of us right around the lead, it's got to be the best chance we've ever had.'

Or the second best. Norman made mistakes. Had a few bad breaks. 'It's just been a steady progression,' Leishman says. 'I started on the secondary tour in Australia and worked my way on to the main tour. I played in Korea. I tried Mondays at the web.com tour in America, won on that tour to get on the main tour there. It's just a slow rise, but taking all the right steps. Not playing on the PGA Tour straight up, you sort of learn how to win a golf tournament. I've done that a few times. I think I've won seven or eight times as a pro now. Slept on the lead at maybe four of them, been close to the overnight lead in a few. So I've sort of done it before.

'Obviously it's different in the Masters, but I feel pretty used to it, to be honest. I actually feel quite comfortable here. I was quite nervous on the first tee on Thursday, a little bit yesterday, not too bad on Saturday. It helps when you're hitting the shots that you want to hit and rolling the putts pretty well. So I'm really looking forward to the last day. Some of the greens are baked and get unbelievably fast. I hit it above the hole by about eight feet on 4 on Saturday. I tried to hit it about three inches and it went about six foot past. It

AMEN

was just like yep, this is what I thought it would be like.'

·· ● ··

Forever Cursed? Craig Parry leads Fred Couples by one shot going into the final round of the 1992 Masters. He's abused and intimidated by hideous spectators who should be thrown off the course for their loathsome behaviour. In an interview on the Saturday night, Parry senses the minefield to come: 'It'll be tough playing with Freddie tomorrow. He's a good friend and usually relaxing to play with, but I know the crowd will be rooting for him. I've just got to play my own game and hope the crowd don't get to me. I know they'll be partisan.'

Parry leads by three after a birdie on the second. Putting for par on the third, he's baulked by a loud cough on his backswing. He stabs at the putt and misses. A burly patron stands in front of Parry and shouts in a threatening if juvenile manner: 'Why don't you let our guy win?' Couples apologises for the ugliness. Parry becomes ragged, posting a 78 before leaving the course close to tears. Alcohol has fuelled the aggressiveness: the place is a zoo. The following morning, Parry says: 'It's not Fred's fault.

He's a gentleman. But I was physically shocked they could want their man to win so badly. I was almost assaulted on the course. I was very upset.'

Ahead of Parry and Couples have been the more demure pairing of Baker-Finch and America's Raymond Floyd. 'If Finchy and I played together, I think one of us would have won,' says Parry. 'We were both playing that good at the time. A little bit of inexperience in majors probably cost me the tournament. Looking back on it, I should have handled it a little bit different. I should have been more focused on the golf course than on what the spectators were doing. I copped a bit. They were influencing my thinking; I was thinking about them rather than trying to win the tournament. I got to three in front and felt as though I was playing all right. It wasn't America versus Australia, but it was just a difficult time because they hadn't had an American win for a while.

'I three-putted the third hole, the fourth hole and the fifth hole. I'd been three in front. Now I'm tied for the lead and I've had three straight three-putts. All the momentum was gone by that stage. Then I clipped the tree on the 10th hole off the tee. It was back in the fairway and I had to play short of MacKenzie's bunker. Then Fred hits it into the creek on 12 and it pops up. If you look at the replay, my marker is a metre and a bit from the hole. His ball goes in the water, I have only a metre and a bit for birdie and all of a sudden it changes again. But it wasn't to be.'

Couples is critical of the gallery and their behaviour. 'On the eighth tee, after we hit, he said wouldn't you love to have a tape recorder to play to these people at the end of the day,' says Parry. 'They were carrying on like school kids. I wouldn't say it was out of control, but they were being very vocal. The following year at the international dinner, I sat next to the head of security and the guy that was in charge of the beer sales. They were going to stop all beer sales if it happened again. That would have been a big call. They changed the drinking hours instead. They pulled it in by an hour for that reason. Jack Nicklaus came up to me and asked me what happened. They knew something was wrong but they didn't know what to do about it, or how to handle it.'

Parry falls to thirteenth. He's such a tidy player, but never again will a winning opportunity present itself. 'You think you're invincible and you feel as though it's going to go on forever,' he says. 'I think I got back there nine times, which is not too bad. It was a golf course that actually didn't suit me. It went right to left, and I hit it left to right.' Of all the people to help Parry put '92 behind him, Ivan Lendl has delivered the most sage advice. The former world No. 1 tennis player won the Australian Open, the US Open and the French Open without securing the one he wanted the most at Wimbledon.

'I played golf with Ivan in Orlando,' says Parry. 'We were at Isleworth, where I'm a member. We were with Wayne Grady and Ivan said, "Can I have your autograph?" I said you have got it all wrong here. He said trust me, I am getting it for my daughter, she watched the Masters last night and you hit it left to right. The golf course is right to left. We started to talk about tennis. I said what was your greatest moment? He said Wimbledon. He said getting to the final of Wimbledon three times was my greatest achievement. He said when I won all the other majors, I was supposed to win and those places actually suited me. He said when you look back at your career and you look back at the Masters, you'll think wow, I played really well that week because it didn't suit me. And he's right. My game is more suited for a British Open where you can hit it low and use your trajectory as an advantage. I should never have been able to play well at Augusta. It was just that I knew my game was pretty good at the time and I got through it. Every time we went there as Australians it was like, okay, who's going to win this week, guys? It was just that the cards hadn't fallen our way.'

Cursed? 'You know, we might win it three times in the next ten years and everyone will say the Australians have a stranglehold on the Masters,' says Baker-Finch. 'But the pressure of trying to win it has built up over those last twenty years with Greg. It has ended up becoming shit, what do we have to do?'

·· ● ··

Sunday, 14 April: The winner will receive US$1.44 million and a replica of Tom Dewey's coat. The third-to-last group is Day and American Matt Kuchar. The second-to-last group is Scott and Leishman, safety in numbers. The final pairing is Angel Cabrera and American Brandt Snedeker. The treasure is the jacket.

Augusta member Toby Wilt is the starter. He asks Cabrera and Snedeker: 'All right, guys. Ready to play a little golf?'

Absolute quiet before the smatterings of applause. Outbreaks of celebrations for the moments of elevated significance. Day starts birdie-eagle. Apparent is the sense of purpose. Umbrellas look like mushroom clouds. Constant voices from the crowd. Come on, now! Scott's pause on his follow-through is the most impressive stationary carriage since *The Thinker.* There's an absence of wild cheering from behind the ropes. More a calm acknowledgement: that is how to hit a golf ball.

The big swinging downhill putts. Scott locks his body into position but the Hills Hoist/winged keel of a putter refuses to attend the party. Weight is jammed on his front foot. The muscles in his left arm are taught. It is a mechanical motion, a prime example of rote learning. All that matters is getting the ball in the hole. You'd lie on the green and hit it with a snooker cue if it worked. Cabrera shovels it around. Such a home-made swing. Such a caddie's swing. Sizing up a putt, Cabrera does that thing where players, mostly of the antique variety, close one eye and hold the shaft of the putter in front of their noses. Leishman attracts polite applause. All very nice. Birds chirp and giggle. Tiger Woods falls from contention.

AMEN

He used to be so good. The jokes used to be so complimentary.

St Peter and Jesus are playing golf in Heaven. Jesus is faced with a shot over water. He asks St Peter, 'What should I hit?' St Peter replies, 'A 5-iron.' Jesus asks what Tiger Woods would hit. St Peter replies, 'An 8-iron.' Jesus pulls out an 8-iron and lands it in the drink. No problem, Jesus walks out on the lake to play his next shot. Moses comes up in the group behind and asks St Peter, 'Who does that guy walking on the water think he is, Jesus Christ?' St Peter says, 'No, that is Jesus Christ. But he thinks he's Tiger Woods.'

We used to laugh because it was kind of true. He really was untouchable. Not anymore. Cabrera's −8 leads them into Amen Corner. The back nine on a Sunday. We are here. The pinnacle of modern golf. Finally the tournament can begin. Moving off the 10th green in their respective groups and moods, Scott, Day and Snedeker are at −6. Leishman is −5, hanging by a thread. Amen Corner constitutes the second shot at the par-four 11th, the tightrope of a tee shot at the par-three 12th and the length and breadth of the par-five 13th. The most famous stretch of holes in golf was without a moniker for 25 under-appreciated years before a golf writer for

Sports Illustrated, Herbert Warren Wind, coined the phrase in 1958. Arnold Palmer had played two balls on the 12th amid a rules controversy before an eagle on 13 helped him win the first of his four Masters by a shot from Doug Ford and Fred Hawkins.

Wrote Wind: 'On the afternoon before the start of the recent Masters golf tournament, a wonderfully evocative ceremony took place at the farthest reach of the Augusta National Course—down in the Amen Corner where Rae's Creek intersects the 13th fairway near the tee, then parallels the front edge of the green on the short 12th and finally swirls alongside the 11th green.' Wind was a jazz buff who claimed to have taken the name from Milton Mezzrow's tune 'Shoutin' In That Amen Corner'. Subsequent research has discovered that Mezzrow never made such a recording. Regardless, the name has stuck for a famous conglomeration of holes.

'I think it's a great conglomeration of circumstances,' says Nicklaus. 'They are all great holes, don't get me wrong. I like all three of them. But you have all the conditions on 11 with the wind, how you play it, and what it does to the golf ball. When you get to 12, if the wind is doing something at 11, it's certainly going to do something else at 12. And you have 13, turning around the corner—the thing is, you've got everybody and their brother watching you play. People can sit there and watch you play all three holes from one location. It's just become such a great focus. There's not many places in golf where you can do that. Hey, he's on 11. Hey, he's on 12, he's over on 13, someone just birdied 11. You're all right there. It's a great thing that's come together.'

Nicklaus has a list of the six most important shots at Augusta. Three of them are at Amen Corner. The tee shot on the par-five second; the approach to the 11th green; the tee shot on the 12th; the tee shot and the second shot on the 13th and the approach or lay-up to the 15th green. Nicklaus still kicks himself over a 3-wood he clunked into the water on the 15th in the final round in 1971.

'One shot shouldn't be a shot that puts you out of the tournament,' he says. 'I needed to make four. I didn't need to make three. I should have laid the ball up. Why put yourself out of the tournament on one shot? That's the thing I stress if someone wants to ask me about the course. I wouldn't take risks unless it was necessary to take risks. These younger guys that come to me, basically what I tell them is there's a half-dozen shots on this golf course where you can put yourself out of the tournament. Think about what you're doing on them. If you've got a 50-50 chance of doing it, certainly I wouldn't be doing it. If you've got a 90-10 chance, think real hard about it, and try to make sure you eliminate the 10. It's a golf course that when you make a mistake, it's really difficult to make up for.'

··•··

'Adam and Steve have a game plan on how to play Amen Corner,' says Phil. 'It's hole by hole, shot by shot. On 11, you just have to make four. It's about hitting the fairway. Playing your shot in, wherever the pin is, if you finish left, you have pulled it. Because you are just wanting to play safe. You just want to get it on the green, even if it is 40 feet, and just try to get four.' Take out one side of the course. Scott gets his four. Twelve is the 157-yard par three. The Masters' postcard. Rae's Creek is in front of the green. A small landing area. No more than a 9-iron or wedge. Bunkers at the back.

'Generally speaking on 12, they will just play by hitting over the bunker, which is the old Nicklaus philosophy there,' says Phil. 'Forget where they put the pin. If you knock it over the middle of the bunker, you never have more than a twenty-foot putt. If you can do that you have taken all the trouble out because we know short is rubbish, the back bunkers are bad. So if you're playing a club you're confident hits the middle of the green, and you aim it over the bunker, if you push it a bit or pull it a bit you're still good.'

Scott goes over the bunker on 12. Sizzles a 9-iron. The swing is almost chivalrous. He makes his three. (Could be worse: defending champion Bubba Watson deposits three balls in Rae's Creek and makes ten.)

'Thirteen is variable subject to conditions,' says Phil. 'If the wind is favourable then a high 3-wood with draw is the desired shot. If it's into wind, the driver comes into the equation. Basically a driver hit straight will run through the fairway into the trees. If there is wind behind, so will a 3-wood. So, basically aiming at the edge of the trees on the inside of the dog leg, high 3-wood with draw is the plan. The result of that dictates the next shot but if the drive is good, it's always on to go for the green in two.'

Thirteen is where Fred Couples hit his most famous shot of all, smoothing a 3-iron, tilting his head just enough to watch it fly with the expression of a fascinated feline. 'Oh, baby,' he purred.

There's absolute dead quiet on the 13th tee because no spectators have access. Just the softest notes of birdsong. The coiled spring, the ball compresses and travels far. Leishman tells Scott: 'Beauty, mate.' From the light rough on the right, he thumps a 7-iron. His ball is between the edge of the fairway and the rope. Commentary from the patrons: Aw, I like it! Eight feet from the pin. It reverses on the downslope, gaining speed as it crosses the painted line that signals the start of the water hazard. The beginning of No Man's Land. And then his ball stops before falling into the water. He chips and putts for a birdie. Highway robbery. One very serious bullet has been dodged. Scott and Day go through Amen Corner in −1. Leishman has three pars. Cabrera trips to +1.

'Thirteen was an interesting one,' says Phil Scott. 'Brad and I were standing on that fairway and we saw Adam's ball all in air. We didn't see him hit it but we saw the ball in the air and we saw it land. We thought it was perfect when it hit that slope behind the pin and started coming back because that's kind of the play you want. So I was

AMEN

a bit surprised when it looked like it would keep going because I thought he had hit just a perfect shot in there. The emotions were one, that's perfect. Two, my God, what is going on? Because Adam is not a massive spinner of the golf ball. The mind goes back to Greg years ago—Adam doesn't do that sort of stuff. I was a bit surprised and then I thought here we go, it's going in the creek. Then it pulled up because the course was a bit wet. The green was a bit softer and the ball reacted a bit more.

'Sunday at the Masters you want to be birdying 13 and 15. Sometimes they're the little bits of luck that just separate your chance of winning from not winning. He didn't hit a crap shot that deserved to go in the creek. So you could argue it was a bit unlucky that it spun that much. And then it was a bit lucky that it stopped. It was important. He needed to make four. He had to make birdie there, and he did. As we saw, Cabrera made six in the group behind and suddenly we're into a whole new ball game.'

·· ● ··

Day birdies 13 and 14. Hoo-ee! He leads the Masters. He will reach the clubhouse first and post the number to chase. He putts for eagle on 15 and this could be the tournament. This could be Day taking a seat at the highest table of Australian sport. The eagle putt is on line, but it's short. Never up . . . still, he leads by two. Scott makes birdie. Day leads by one. Leishman finds the water and this will be a bridge too far for him. Just a small bridge. Cabrera's swing is going haywire. Day goes long with his tee shot at the par-three 16th, landing where Woods chipped in from in 2005, his ball stopping right on the lip, showing the Nike logo at the cameras, flashing its smile and swan-diving into the hole. No bells and whistles here: Day bogeys and delivers an incongruous smile. 'That's just a coping mechanism, maybe,' he says. 'If I smile and try to enjoy myself when I hit bad shots, I won't be so disappointed.'

Scott is 178 yards away on the tee. Another commanding swing. Look at it. Steve Williams tells him: 'Perfect.' Ball lands where the form guide says it must. To the right of the pin. High and mighty. The roars in the valley of the 16th are off the scale when a ball is creeping towards the hole. The ball itself becomes the star of the show, willed along and inspired by the noise, leaving Scott with a ten-footer to tie the lead.

AMEN

Patrons are heckling one another. Put your umbrella down. No one can see. Scott misses on the low side, the amateur side. Such an opportunity. Playoff with Day? Do their merry dance? Have an old-fashioned shootout for the asterisk? Cabrera sneaks a decent tee shot onto the 16th green—and drains the putt and from nowhere, there's a three-way tie for the lead again. An old wives' tale at Augusta says if you birdie 16, you win the tournament. The luck or the coincidence. Or maybe it's already written? Old wives' tales should be taken with a grain of salt at Augusta National: old wives have rarely been allowed in. Day keeps to his pre-shot routine, closing his eyes and visualising the swing and flight of the ball to come. Searching for his Mooshan state. The peace and calm and quiet. Conquer this place and you conquer the world.

Day is in pole position on the 17th fairway. Without saying a word to Col Swatton, he changes clubs at the last minute, ditching his 7-iron for an 8-iron. Not a word of consultation with his coach and caddie and then the approach falls short. What a mistake. He should have stuck with the 7. Long may he regret the change of heart. Echoes of Norman versus Nicklaus, the uncertainty with the club selection, the error in judgement. A second straight bogey. He nearly pokes his eye with his umbrella. Everything has become disjointed.

Rain is tumbling when Scott hits another pearl to the 17th green. The pleading eyes. He needs his ball to stay on the same plateau as the pin. It does. Cabrera clubs his drive. Order has been restored: he no longer seems at risk of falling flat on his face on his follow-through. Scott's birdie putt is right in the heart of the cup and there's a booming voice in the crowd: Queenslander! But it's short. There can be no greater letdown. Scott exhales, deeply. Cabrera ambles up to the green and we have the heartwarming sight of his son, Angel Jr, on the bag. Suffice it to say, he did not abandon him at the age of two. A silken putt from Cabrera. One tiny break to the right and . . . it stays high! Cabrera is feeling this. The moment and the opportunity. Day pars the last and tells Col Swatton: 'I should have won.'

He's incredulous under thunderhead clouds. 'I love this tournament regardless of where I finish,' says Day. 'It's obviously an honour to come this week and play against the best players in the world, and obviously having a shot at winning my first major and being the first Australian to win the Masters.

AMEN

There's a lot of experience that I can take into next year and hopefully I can wear one of those green jackets soon. If you can have a shot in most majors, sooner or later you're going to get one. I can't look at the week as a disappointment. Obviously I'd love to wear the green jacket because I've been dreaming about it since I was a kid. I think I've just got to take the experience and keep going on. I'm happy with whoever wins, because they have done the work and they have worked very hard to get here and they have played four great rounds of golf. I'm really pulling for Scotty, though, because I know he's come close so many times in majors. He's worked very hard and he really does deserve it.'

Only two men are standing. Scott and Cabrera. When Scott likes a shot, when he really likes it, he starts chewing on his tongue. He likes his 8-iron from 161 yards to the 18th green. He likes it because it's going to leave him with the O'Meara Putt. He steps into the fairytale, gives his Titleist a promising roll, patrons in the background, everything as it should be. Day tells CBS: 'It's really tough. Pressure got to me a little bit. But I'm very happy for Adam right now. I hope he follows through and wins the thing.'

The putt hits the edge of the cup . . . pause . . . and lips in. This is Adam Scott Unplugged. This is Adam Scott letting it all hang out. He high-fives his caddie with brute strength and roars about being an Australian. This is Adam Scott charging around the 18th green while fist-pumping the crowd. He had the putt he always craved. He made it. Now he places his hand on his umbrella and sighs with the satisfaction of a man who might just have completed his life's work. The man who has applied the last full stop to his manuscript. The man who just might have written *The Great Australian Novel*. He slaps hands with patrons on his charge to the scorers' tent. The BBC asks: 'Are the Fosters ready?'

Scott should put an exclamation mark next to his three. A three! Yet there is a rider to the putt. He could not, in all conscience and honesty, tell himself *This to win the Masters*. Because Cabrera can match his birdie and enforce the playoff.

The Argentine hears the loudest single roar of the week. From the fairway, he watches Scott's salutations. His task has been simplified. Make a birdie. That's it. Cabrera takes command. 'Quiet, please!' He yells it out himself. The lumberjack's forearms. Strong contact with the ball. He rocks back on his

Four Australians contest the 2013 Masters: Adam Scott, Jason Day, Mark Leishman and John Senden (pictured). (Harry How/Getty Images)

Jason Day knows what he wants: the World No. 1 ranking: 'You can't blame a guy for trying to be the best at his profession.' (Don Emmert/AFP/Getty Images)

Believe in omens? Adam Scott has already birdied the first hole of the Masters from a fairway trap. Now comes the three-day battle to keep his name on Augusta's white leader boards until Sunday afternoon. (Jim Watson/AFP/Getty Images)

Angel Cabrera (here with Brandt Snedeker, right) of Argentina has gone from being a caddie to being the US Open and US Masters champion. 'The journey has been a long, long winding road for him,' says his coach, Charlie Epps. 'He has done himself proud.' (Harry How/Getty Images)

Above: One cup or two? Adam Scott and caddie Steve Williams. Scott's ball has only just steered clear of Rae's Creek during The Back Nine On a Sunday. 'That stuff, you can't control it,' he says. 'I think the golfing gods sort all those things out.' (Andrew Redington/Getty Images)

Left: The putting, the putting, the putting. Adam Scott piles one birdie chance on top of another in the final round at Augusta. On the seventeenth green, with time and holes running out, another opportunity slips by. (David Cannon/Getty Images)

Above: Angel Cabrera, with his son as caddie, makes an immaculate birdie under excruciating pressure on the 72nd hole to force a playoff against Adam Scott. 'I know his state of mind,' says Charlie Epps. 'He's his own man because he's been on his own since he was two years old.' Say what? 'His mum and dad, they gave him away to his grandmother. So he grew up without a mum and dad.' (Andrew Redington/ Getty Images)

Left: Tiger Woods is without a major triumph since the 2008 US Open. (Andrew Redington/ Getty Images)

Left: The Hills Hoist of a putter. The winged keel of a putter. The cure for all that ails him. 'He's a great athlete and it freed him from his old thoughts,' says his coach, Brad Malone. (Harry How/ Getty Images)

Below: Amen Corner swings through the 11th, 12th and 13th holes at Augusta National. A great conglomeration of holes? 'I think it's a great conglomeration of circumstances,' says Nicklaus. (Jamie Squire/ Getty Images)

Adam Scott wins the Masters when he holes his birdie putt at the 72nd hole. Or so he thinks. He would have to do it again in a thriller of a playoff with Angel Cabrera. (Andrew Redington/Getty Images)

Facing page: History: an Australian wins the Masters. 'The winning putt might be the highlight putt of my career,' says Scott's caddie, Steve Williams. 'Because he asked me to read it.' (Andrew Redington/Getty Images)

Left: Scott hugs Cabrera after their playoff. 'You know, Angel is a great man . . . he said a great thing to me [in 2009 at the Presidents Cup] . . . I was on a captain's pick there and my form was struggling, but he pulled me aside and he said, "You are a great, great player." It was something I wouldn't forget.' (Andrew Redington/Getty Images)

Below: The green jacket is all. Scott receives the emperor's new clothes from American Bubba Watson. 'It's incredible to be in this position,' he says. 'I'm honoured . . . it's amazing that it's my destiny.' (Ross Kinnaird/Getty Images)

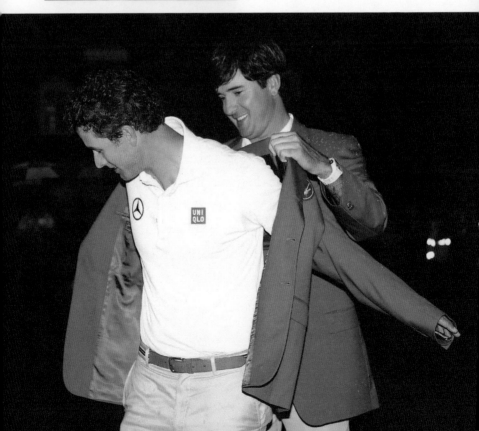

heels and then marches forward, talking to the ball like he yelled at the patrons. Get close. How will a 3 go here? Be right. It is.

Scott has his head down in the tent: he is checking off his score card when Cabrera's die is cast. Another phenomenal roar. Golf is all about producing the big shot under the most extreme pressure. Scott looks up and to the left. One small TV screen is on the wall. He watches the ball hit and stick. Two feet from the pin. He goes back to his scorecard as though nothing untoward has happened. He tells Williams they must prepare for their return to work. Cabrera still has to sink his putt. They're never as easy as they seem. He aims for the right edge. He hugs his boy and it's beautiful. We are playoff-bound. Scott's high has lasted all of eight minutes.

'Adam hit an awesome shot into 15, probably about 20 feet away,' says Brad Malone. 'He really had to do something at this point. I'm thinking if this is going to be your week, Ad, this putt would certainly help. He didn't hole it. At which point Jason made a four at 16. Then Adam hit another good shot into 16. He just kept hitting the shots. They're going down 17 tied for the lead. I was up the 17th fairway, where Jason was hitting from. I thought, gee, Jason is in good position here. He came up short, in the bunker, and unfortunately made bogey. Adam struck it up the fairway, in basically the same position as Jason. I thought to myself, just keep hitting the shots, you never know. They go up 18, Adam again hitting the fairway, hitting the green, giving himself a chance at the putt. It's one of those putts you would have hit so many times in your mind. It's the putt O'Meara has holed. Tiger has holed it. Mickelson has holed it to win. Adam hits a great putt, holes it and at that point, he's so excited and pumped that he shows his emotions. But this is where golf is not over until it's over. Cabrera hits and he stiffs it. It wasn't even a question of whether there would be a playoff. He was going to make that putt. You know it's time to focus again. You know it's far from over.'

'On 13, from back on the fairway, it looked like Scotty's ball had stopped on the green,' says Leishman. 'I think I said good shot. Scotty had the putter out walking up to the green. All of a sudden it's rolling back down the hill. We're like, oh no. The rain definitely saved him there. That hill doesn't look steep on TV but it's *really* steep. It would be well more than 45 degrees. Well more. If you tried to walk down there you would slip straight over and land on your butt. I think the rain and a bit of moisture on the grass kept his ball up. He hit a good chip and holed a fairly tough putt down the hill to make the birdie and capitalise on it. In the long run that was probably the break. You look at Fred Couples in '92 when his ball stayed up. That was the same.

'On the 16th tee, I was thinking if I birdied the last three, I was still a chance. I hit a great putt on 16 and it sat on the edge. That was when I probably thought my chances were gone unless I did something miraculous and holed my second shot on 17. Walking up the 17th fairway, I think Adam and Cabrera were maybe one or two ahead of Jase. That's when I thought we needed Scotty to bring it home for us. I didn't say anything to him about winning. I just made sure I was near him when we were walking between shots. Because if I was in that position, the last thing I would want would be to walk along having no one to talk to, thinking about nothing.

'I can't even remember what we were talking about. We would have been talking crap about something. We're both reasonably sarcastic people, I would say. We really were just talking crap walking up 17 and 18. I think it was good that he had someone there with him who could do that. I'm not saying he wouldn't have won if he wasn't playing with an Australian. But I'm saying it was easier for him to relax with a friend close to him, I guess. We've had dinner a couple of times. I wouldn't say we're close-close mates but we're friends, definitely. If he's there at lunch, I'll sit down and have lunch with him. We're mates. I think we had lunch one day at Augusta. I can't remember what day it would have been. You walk past, have a chat and away you go because obviously you both want to win.'

Leishman has the best seat in the house for the putt on 18. He received one of Scott's bone-jarring acknowledgements. 'Huge,' he says. 'Definitely made the hair on the back of my neck stand up. His reaction, and to be there to celebrate with him, was incredible. Obviously I was wanting one of my mates to win the Masters. Then that shot Cabrera hit into 18 after Scotty's putt was unbelievable. To be able to do it in that situation, under that pressure was brilliant. It was hard not to think "Oh no, not again." I was going to hang around for the finish but once the playoff was there, I left. Adam would have two or three hours of media commitments when he finished and I wouldn't be able to see him anyway.'

Leishman can hold his head high. 'It was a great week for me to be leading the Masters after the first round,' he says. 'Then to stay right there all week until a couple of holes to go, it's been a big week. To finish fourth after the first few months of the year I had—things were okay without being great. I was still on antibiotics the whole week. But I know there's a lot of people feeling a lot worse than I've been. Great week. Hopefully it will work out for the best with Scotty. Obviously it didn't work out the way I wanted it to for me today, but I had a great tournament and it's something to build on. I know I can put it together for four rounds. Probably a lot of guys didn't expect me to do what I did. I didn't finish off the way I would have liked, but I have a lot of positives to take away from it. Hopefully it's going to be a great tournament for Australians. I hope that Scotty can pull it off in the playoff. I'm not sure exactly what Jason finished on, but hopefully he's going to be in the top five. And hopefully it's about to end with us standing around with Scotty wearing the green jacket.'

The sweet exhaustion of it all. 'I was surprisingly relaxed all week,' he says. 'I slept really good every night. Probably the worst I slept was Sunday night after it was done. But I was fine. Mum and Audrey were cooking every night. I was playing with my son, Harvey, at night. Having everyone there just to relax was good. I'm a pretty laidback person and so is my family. I was surrounded by the people I wanted to be surrounded by.

'Probably the most nervous I was all week was on the first tee on Thursday. After that I was pretty calm. We didn't tee off until 2.30 p.m. on the last day—it was a long wait. I probably slept in until nine o'clock. I played with Harvey for a bit just to amuse him. Headed out the course about twelve o'clock.

'It was really relaxed. If you had of said that to me five years ago, if you had said to me that you're going to be one or two behind going into the last round of the Masters, I would have been shitting myself. For sure. But I felt like I belonged. Mostly because I was playing good golf. I was hitting shots I wanted to hit, I was putting well and that's why you do all the practice your whole life to get into that situation. I was finally there.'

Paul Leishman finds himself in unfamiliar territory. 'There was a lot of media for Marc,' he says. 'I said to his manager, Bud, tell Marc I'll meet him in the car park. Bud said you can't miss this. I ended up in Butler Cabin while Marc was being interviewed. It was amazing—eye-opening for me. I did a fair few interviews as well. I guess a lot of people thought he would go away. But to be on the first page virtually all week, he got a lot out of that. Watching the first nine was okay, but once we got down to his second shot into 10 it was very hard to see. From there on it was really hard because once it started raining, people put their umbrellas up. I was going on crowd reaction. On 16 I really didn't see anything. I was probably fifteen people back in the crowd. After 16 it was pretty much done. And then on 18, I was there but I couldn't see anything. I remember when Scotty holed that putt, it was the biggest roar I have ever heard. It was sensational. We were all over there waiting for them to come out of the scorer's hut when Scotty signed his card. Marc said as soon as Cabrera birdied 18, Scotty just said to Steve, "Righto, come on, we have golf to play." Marc said that was so impressive because he would have been on the biggest high. He would have been thinking he had already won it.'

·· ● ··

Scott sits in a golf cart at the business end of Magnolia Lane, near the Founders' Circle roundabout in front of the clubhouse. It's an incredibly sullen scene of rain and solitude. Scott is told that Cabrera needs time to sign his card. He climbs out of his cart and steps onto the clubhouse porch, staring vacantly at the falling drops. He picks at his cuticles. In a different cart, Steve Williams is still in his jumpsuit, flicking through his yardage book. Solemnity. It's beyond belief given the ear-piercing celebrations that have only just finished. Adam Scott has won nothing yet. He may finish the day with the joy of holing the dream putt on the 72nd hole . . . but still not winning the Masters. He needs to do it twice. When Cabrera's ball has landed next to the 18th pin in the ultimate twist to the plot, Norman has texted his mates: 'The golf gods can't be this cruel to Australia.' He knows they can.

·· ● ··

The First Playoff Hole. 'He'd gone straight in to sign his scorecard after his round,' says Malone. 'I was in the clubhouse then. I wanted to make sure Cabrera holed out. I wandered back out and they were already going down to the 18th. We went down behind the green. To see them both standing there in the middle of the fairway—I think the biggest thing for me was that through the entire final round of golf, Adam just hit shot after shot that was quality. He was so patient. When it really mattered the first time on 18, he gave himself a chance and he holed it. But he had to be even more patient.'

Epps is zig-zagging through all of Augusta's fairways, trees, wind tunnels and secret chambers. 'I followed Angel every hole,' he says. 'I don't miss anything. When he finished 17 in the regular round, I walked up and got behind the 18th green. As soon as I got there, and it was a good spot, I saw Adam's putt and all the emotion. I could honestly say, okay guys, this isn't over. In that situation, I knew he could handle it. He's done it before. He's won more than 40 tournaments worldwide. He's won two majors. He's won the Masters. He was hitting the ball really well, so why not expect the best?

'I watched him from afar: he went through his routine and I saw him strike the shot. I count one thousand, one thousand one, one thousand two, one thousand three. By then I know the ball is about ready to land. He stuck it. I was so, so proud. But I wasn't surprised. He was very, very into the moment for the playoff. Very, very focused, in the zone. He wasn't distracted by anything. We got into a cart and they drove us back down to the 18th tee. He won the Masters in a playoff so he had been through this before.'

More, more. The encore. They're both short of the 18th green for two. Cabrera likes the look of his chip. Not again. He nearly does a Mize. Not again! 'My heart went into my mouth,' says Epps. 'Angel thought he made it. He was hitting pretty chips all week long.'

Scott knocks his close without threatening to sink it. Cabrera makes four. Scott has a four-footer to stay in it. The ultimate test of nerves. Nothing to gain. All you can do is draw level again. There are two ways to hole a short putt under throat-constricting circumstances: in a state of knee-trembling distress, or with a firmness of hand and technique. Straight in the hole. The playoff moves to the 10th, a plummeting par four that starts high and ends in the basement.

'I was down there with Phil,' says Brad Malone.

'One of the committee members was nice enough to let us jump inside the rope so we could see the green from about 100 yards out. We knelt down at the side there.'

From the fairway. Cabrera is first. One one thousand . . . two one thousand . . . three one thousand . . . the Argentinian's ball nestles 15 feet from the pin. Scott dials his to 12 feet. *This* is the shot. Under the immense pressure of Cabrera already being on the green, Scott's reply has been resolute. He looks over to Cabrera—and his old mate from the Presidents Cup is giving him a thumbs up.

'Angel doesn't wish anybody bad, ever,' says Epps. 'He's a deep-down wonderful person and now that he is a grandfather, even more so. That was a class act.'

Both of them have birdie putts for the loot. Masters officials have taken two jackets out of the closet: the one that Cabrera won in 2009. And another that will fit Scott. If Scott wins, he will wear the untailored jacket for the presentation in Butler Cabin. Then he will be measured and a new jacket will be made to order. Masters champions are allowed to take the jacket with them for one year. Before the start of the following year's tournament, it must be returned. Multiple champions only receive one jacket, their first. They may apply for another if they fatten up or shrink in old age. Cabrera's stroke is beautiful. The camera flashes! Might go in! Has to go in! It shaves the right edge. Sheesh. If you know golf, you know that putt could have dropped as easily as it missed. Cabrera taps in for his four. And then a roar for Adam Scott.

This is really it. This is the real dream sequence. This is the absolutely impossible moment you can seek for decades and suddenly . . . it's here? Behind Scott's right shoulder is a towering pine in the shape of a V. He crouches to map the ball's journey. Twelve feet! That is all.

Steve Williams moves close to whisper a secret. One cup or two?

·· ● ··

If the Putt Goes In . . . 'When Cabrera missed I thought, "Wow, this is the first putt Adam's had in his life to win a major championship,"' Brad Malone will say. 'At the Open, he never had a putt to win. This was his first chance. To see him line it up with Steve, and just make a beautiful stroke at

AMEN

it, and then to see it go in—that point right there was the absolute pinnacle. You knew he had won it. There was nothing anyone could do to take it away from him. All the hard work had paid off and the reaction was just incredible. Everyone was leaping around, I'd never seen Phil jump as high.

'I tell you, it was the most excited I have ever been at a sporting event. More excited than when I was playing myself. Just a huge rush of emotions. I managed to get down and give him a hug and tell him how good that was. Plain awesome, really. I said to him, gee, Adam, you're just a champion. Having been on the journey with him, from seeing him at the low points, to seeing him nearly win the Masters in 2011 and handing a major away in 2012, to knowing what you go through as a player, and how hard you continue to push and work— what the spectator sees is four or five hours of golf every day. What really, really goes into it is hours and hours off the course. You give your heart and soul to the game. You give it your life. Everybody believed in him and it was one of those tournaments where he did everything he needed to and when he had his chance, he took it.'

·· ● ··

If the Putt Goes In . . . 'He was always going to be the best,' says Baker-Finch. 'Having had a special interest in the man over the years, it's rewarding to see. It was very emotional. When he holed the putt and screamed out "Come on, Aussie!" I was really choked up. Then we had to regroup because Angel birdied the last. I was still choked up and had tears. I would have been emotional with any Australian victory because I like all the boys. Jason Day is a future champion and Marc Leishman really proved to us that he has something special. But Adam was who I thought would win. I thought Tiger was going to be the champion leading into the event but Adam was always in my top five.

'That's often the way it works: you mess up a major then win it the next year. I'm just incredibly proud of him. I hope I don't get into trouble for saying this, but I was in touch with Greg on a regular basis throughout the afternoon. We were texting each other back and forth. It was a gut-wrenching moment, to be honest, when Cabrera hit that shot on 18. We said that when it happened. Greg texted me and said mate, let's channel every bit of positive energy we can into Adam. Let's get him through this. It's time an Australian won. It was an emotional time. I texted Greg when he holed the putt and said mate, I'm all choked up. I think I said I had a tear in my eye. Greg said me, too: tears in my eyes.'

••●••

If the Putt Goes In . . . 'My son called me up on the Sunday afternoon and said, "You watching this?"' Norman will say. 'I said of course I'm watching it. He came over and we sat and watched the last six holes together. Probably drank about three beers per hole. A little nervous. I'm over the moon. I spoke to Adam and I said, "Look, now I know how other people felt when they were watching me." I mean, I was a wreck. An absolute wreck, and I've never been like that. I don't get tied up emotionally in things in life, but Adam got me there. Yes, there was a tear. Maybe more than one.'

Why the involvement all these years? 'Part of the responsibility of being at the pinnacle of what-ever you do is that you have to give back. A lot of people gave me that. Jack Nicklaus gave me that. Raymond Floyd, Tom Watson—I could go down the list of guys who reached out to me when I was trying to get to my pinnacle. And I'm no different now with guys coming through. Jason Day, same thing. Marc Leishman, same thing. I've reached out to those guys. If they call me, I'm always going to call them back. But I've had a very close relationship with Adam for a long time, so I probably have a closer connection to him than Jason and Marc and obviously I was happier for him. It was like watching my own son win the golf tournament, to tell you the truth.

'That's how I felt. It's important for Australian golf because we need a shot in the arm. It's been languishing since the economy turned around in 2007, maybe even before that. It's seemingly been a little bit in the doldrums but now, because of Adam, hopefully it will start kicking back up and the energy will get back into Australian golf. If it does, Adam is going to have to be the tip of the spear. He's put himself out there, and I'm proud of him for that. But he has to keep it going forward, which he will. He knows what he has to do. I'm happy for him and the country.

'There was a chance there of three Australians being in a playoff for our first green jacket. There could only be one winner and it probably should have been Jason Day. Could have, should have, but it wasn't. That's golf and Adam will win a lot more now. The guy has confidence from this that will last him for, well, a long time, maybe forever. He's old enough to be able to handle the heartaches of life. He has the maturity to come back from things like the British Open. He has a wealth of information and experience.'

• • ● • •

If the Putt Goes In . . . Phil will bask in this day of days. 'Sunday morning was a bit of fun at the house,' he will say. 'We were all watching highlights and a lot of the talk was obviously about the Woods thing, the Woods debacle. There wasn't any specific talk pre-round about let's go win the Masters. It was let's go do another day and get into it. Brad and I walked together for the day, which we like doing. It's difficult because there are so many people coming up to you, wishing you well and talking about stuff. We don't like getting too much in front. We just like to watch the golf and whatever talk there is, it's just the two of us.

'It's actually quite hard because you want to be nice to everyone. You know their intent is great but you're almost wishing you were on your own.

There's the Aussie journos, people in the industry—they're all great because Adam is quite popular and the Aussies in the crowd are buzzing anyway because with three Australians on the leader board, surely somebody has to win it. That's hard for me because it's right. An Australian probably is going to win it—and I want it to be Adam. With all respect to Jason or Leish, I don't want them to win. That's just being honest.

'So we just walked around and kind of kept pace with Adam and Leish. You're trying to be calm. And it is all pretty calm until about 12 or 13 and then as we know, that's when it all starts moving. Jason makes a couple of birdies. Adam makes a birdie or two. Cabrera makes the unfortunate six on 13. You keep looking at the boards around and thinking well, this is getting serious. He really is a chance here. It was bucketing down with rain, when Brad and I were standing on the 15th, and we got caught on the cross-over. They didn't open the ropes at the time we thought they would, so we were stuck. It was just after Adam had hit his drive and we were trying to get across to the right-hand side of 15. They wouldn't let us.

'We could see Jason on 16. I could see where he

hit it on 16 as Adam got to playing his second shot on 15. It would be untrue to say at that point you're not a bit tense. You're thinking Adam has to make four on 15 or it's too much. Then when we saw where Jason hit it on 16, we know it's not a good spot. Adam hit a lovely iron shot into 15 and ten minutes later, everything has changed. Jason bogeys 16, Adam birdies and they're back together. Fifteen minutes later Jason bogeys 17 and by now you're really thinking it's getting interesting. It's tense and all Brad and I were trying to do was keep calm. We were saying we just wanted Adam to hit the shots. I think we probably both had the inner belief that if he hit the shots, he would be fine.

'We go scuttling up the hill at 18. It's not the easiest thing to get up that hill. By now most of southern America is there. As we came up on the left Adam had hit his second shot. We couldn't get a spot to see the putt. So we said let's run into the grill room and watch it on the telly. That's what we did. We got ourselves right at the back of the room. Obviously we were pretty excited when it went in. We knew as we walked in there that he was tied with Cabrera. So while we were excited it went in and he was ahead, of course we know it's all coming down to what Cabrera does. Brad and I had a bit of a giggle about it.

'After Adam holed his putt, we said we know it's not the right thing to wish bad on someone. That's not the way to go. I said to Brad, "Well, it's not unfair to wish him a nice, rock-solid par. That would be okay". Then he stiffs it and you think oh God. Immediately we were saying we hoped Adam was ready to go again. We later found out they were. Steve and Adam did a very good job of coming off that high. By the time he was in the scorer's hut, they had talked about getting ready to play. I didn't see him before the playoff. I saw him quickly after the first hole of it, walking from the 18th green to 10. I just looked at him. He caught my eye and sort of half-nodded. He looked as though he was in the zone.

'It was fairly nervy watching 18 during the playoff. No one talks much about it but that sort of four-footer doesn't look that easy when it's to keep it alive. I thought he hit a super putt there. It was a confident looking putt to me. For the 10th, the Masters people had asked us if we wanted to go into Butler Cabin to watch it. We said no, we would rather stay out on the course. Well, we couldn't get down 10. Happily, they were very nice to us and scooted us down the 18th fairway. We cut through the trees on the right of 18, back to 10.

'They said you can go anywhere you like, so we went inside the ropes. About 60 yards short of the green, there's a big tree on the right and we stood under that. But I couldn't see the ball on the green. That was the level of darkness. I watched the crowd when they putted. So when Cabrera putted, I watched the through-line crowd. My heart did flip-flops there because the crowd went up, thinking it was going in. Then they all sat down with the groan, so happy days. There was no through-line crowd from where Adam putted on the left of 10, so I thought I would watch Adam and the crowd on the right.

'I know in Adam's putting, if he doesn't move at all on the follow-through when the putter has finished its swing, then I know it means it has started on the line he chose. I saw him do that and thought, well, he has hit it where he thought he should hit it. Then I swung my eyes to the right and looked at the crowd. It felt like ten seconds. I guess it's a second and a half. Then I saw them go up, and I heard the noise. Brad and I were jumping and hugging. It's a bit surreal, isn't it. Then I scuttled down. It was wet.'

No running allowed!

'I was walking,' he says. 'I still had the thing in my mind that I better not run. They don't like running. So I wandered down, by which time he had done all his bits on the 10th. He was just getting off the green when I got there. It was a great moment. I just said to him literally, no matter what happens from here, it will never get better than this. He said much the same sort of thing. It was brilliant, it honestly was. It's hard to put into words. I was just over the moon. In hindsight, it feels like he just gave me the greatest gift. My whole life has been golf. To watch my son win the Masters is just unbelievable.'

To Butler Cabin. 'Brad and I were saturated,' says Phil. 'We went and got a cup of tea and Adam was downstairs in the cabin, doing the TV scene which we watched on TV. We didn't see Adam for probably an hour and a half by the time he did the TV, outdoor ceremony and then the press conference. I knew what he had to do. Frankly, after about half an hour, all I wanted to do was change clothes and make a proper cup of tea. They're not big on tea in America. After I got a cup of green tea with milk in it, I said to the guy, "Just let me make the tea."

'There's a big dinner, so happily we were able to change our clothes. Billy Payne told me what was going on for the night so we basically just tagged along. After the dinner Adam had to do about another hour of TV. It wrapped up about 11.45 p.m. The dinner is just mingles. It's not formal. Adam just wandered around with the members. Steve went back to the house and brought Jay back. There were about 200 there. It was certainly after midnight when we got back to the house. It was only a pretty minor celebration. Had a couple of beers. Wrapped up about three-ish. We had a bit of a chat and then wandered off to bed about four. I gave up at five. Came back down. Adam was down soon after. He had given up trying to sleep. Brad came down. He had given up. So we all just had a cup of tea, bit of brekkie and by 9.30 it was time to hit the road. I went to Monterrey and played golf for three days.'

·· ● ··

If the Putt Goes In . . . 'I knew he was going to make it,' Charlie Epps will say. 'It was destiny. You could just see it. He had the aid of a caddie that had won there before. He was given a good read and made one hell of a putt. I was happy for him. After suffering so badly at the British Open—a lot of guys don't recover from that. There's a lot of guys in history who've gone down to the wire, lost and they can't recover. To see someone come back from what happened at the Open, and for that man to be Adam, I couldn't have been happier. I really couldn't. Angel had done all he could.

'It reminded me of Jack Nicklaus and Tom Watson at Turnberry in '77. Or Nicklaus at Pebble Beach when Watson chipped in and beat him again. Nicklaus was always gracious in defeat. At that time, the true man comes out. That's what I liked. That people could see that a poor kid from Argentina could do things the right way. I just said to Angel, man, you played so well and it was such a great day. We did the press conferences and went up to the Champions Room. He and his manager and I sat there. Not much was said. We had a little cocktail, gathered ourselves. We went to the car and reminisced a little bit, but not much was said. We got home and a few of the guys were there and we had a nice quiet evening. You don't celebrate. Angel always says that the person in second is the first person who loses. But deep-down he knew he didn't lose. He got beaten, and there's a difference.

'One shot I think is going to get lost is Angel's shot into the 13th off the pine straw. He knew the guys ahead of him were making birdies. You don't win Augusta by laying up. He hit a beautiful shot, but it started two yards wide of where he wanted it to be, and it drifted. His ball went down into the creek but Adam's stayed up. When he saw what happened to Adam's ball on the replay, he said, "Oh my gosh, look at that." But he was in the fray and played aggressive all week long. You can't ask for anything more.'

·· ● ··

If the Putt Goes In . . . 'The winning putt might be the highlight putt of my career,' Steve Williams will say. 'Because he asked me to read it.'

·· ● ··

If the Putt Goes In . . . you will be ushered to Butler Cabin for the fireside presentation . . .

Jim Nantz: 'Adam, what a riveting, incredible day, and at long last you are a major champion and Australia is going to be wearing the green jacket here in just a moment. How do you put into words how you finished today, with the birdie at the 72nd hole and then a birdie to win on the second playoff hole?'

You: 'I don't know how that happens. It seems a long way away from a couple of years ago here and even last July, when I was trying to win another major. It fell my way today. There was some luck there somewhere. I don't know how to digest it all at the moment, but it was incredible. It's incredible to be in this position. I'm honoured.'

Jim Nantz: 'Well as you know, the whole world is watching this right now. I can only imagine what it's like in Australia. You think of how long that country has starved to have a Masters champion. You think of all the great players who came before you, who have their fingerprints on your career. What do you have to say about that? Do you feel their presence here?'

You: 'Well, absolutely. I tried not to think about anything today along those lines. The thing I did well out there was just staying right where I was. Wherever it was on the golf course, I stayed in that one shot. Australia is a proud sporting nation and this is one notch in the belt we never got. Amazing that it's come down to me today, Marc and Jason Day—it could have been any one of us. But there's one guy who inspired a nation of golfers and that's Greg Norman. He's been incredible to me and all the young golfers in Australia. Part of this definitely belongs to him.'

Jim Nantz: 'I can only imagine how proud he is right now. And then to make the putt at the 72nd and to think you have won the Masters at that point, to have to go out and earn it all over again, how hard was that to do?'

You: 'Well, it was a split second I thought I'd won. You should never count your chickens. But that was the putt we've seen so many guys make to win. That's what I thought. It's time for me to step up and see how much I want this. To make a couple of putts to win the Masters is just an amazing feeling.'

Jim Nantz: 'It does change your career. It really does. That green jacket is about to be on your shoulders. Billy, it's that time.'

Billy Payne: 'Bubba, if you'd do the honours.'

If the putt goes in, Adam Scott will take a deep breath . . . and slide into his size 40 Regular.

'Oh.'

•• • ••

The Emotion: 'What an incredible day,' Scott will say if the putt goes in. 'Everything fell my way in the end, I guess. You just never know. I just kept plugging away. I didn't know if it was going to happen through nine. But a good back nine here solves a lot and gives you a chance. Eighteen, I was pumped. It was a huge moment. That was the one, I felt I had to seize it right there. This is the chance, put all the pressure on the guy back down the fairway. So I was really pumped and I felt like this was my chance and I took it. And then, you know, incredible support. I felt there were a lot of Australians out there all week, but incredible support from everyone in the crowd. I really felt they were on my side a little bit in regulation, coming down the last couple of holes.

'They wanted me to do something and that's a great feeling. I didn't want to disappoint them. I wanted the moment to happen. Then going to the playoff was a special feeling. Going down the 10th fairway was almost deafening, and the crowd wasn't close. It was a great feeling and I felt like they were really, really pulling for me out there. You know, that is a nice feeling to have when you're trying to hit some shots at that point. It's just great that everything fell into place for me, and I'm just so proud of myself and everyone around me who has helped. The list is so long that I can't do thank-yous. But I'm a proud Australian and I hope this sits really well back at home, even in New Zealand. We had the trans-Tasman combo out there with Steve on the bag. It's hard to put it all together in my mind at the moment, but it's just a real honour. Amazing that Dad was here. A hug with him behind the 10th green when it was all over is something I will never forget.'

The National Pride: 'I guess when I get home I'll find out,' Scott will say if the putt goes in. 'Golf is a big sport at home. It may not be the biggest, but it's a sport that's been followed with a long list of great players, and this was one thing in golf that we had not been able to achieve. So it's amazing that it's my destiny to be the first Aussie to win. Just incredible.' He is reminded of his loudest exclamation. 'Come on, Aussie. Yeah, that's right. I did yell that out. It was maybe a natural reaction. That's from back in my cricket days probably. I don't know if Steve appreciated me yelling that straight towards him, but whatever. Maybe the one time he doesn't mind.'

The Norman Effect: 'He inspired a nation of golfers, anyone near to my age, older and younger.

He was the best player in the world and he was an icon in Australia. He's devoted so much time to myself and other young Australian players who came after him. Incredibly generous. Most of us would feel that he could have slipped a green jacket on, and I said part of this is for him because he's given me so much time and inspiration and belief. I drew on that a lot today. I haven't had time to think about what I'll say to him, I haven't had time to think about anything—but hopefully at some point I'll get to sit down with Greg and have a chat and go through it all. I'm sure he's really happy. A phone conversation isn't going to do it for us. We're really close, and I'd love to share a beer with him over this one.'

The Delayed Sense of Destiny: 'If you're referring to 13, I definitely didn't think it then,' he will say if the putt goes in. 'There was so much golf to go and I had no momentum on the day at that point. I was trying to get something to happen. That was a great break and everyone who wins gets those kinds of breaks—not everyone, but that was a good one to have. I made my four. But even going down 15, I really felt like it was far away still. Jason was looking very much in control and I was just trying to go about my business. On 18, for a split second, I let myself think I could have won. Might have showed that when it went in. But you know, I got to see Angel hit an incredible shot from the scorer's area, and then it was about trying to get myself ready to play some more holes.'

The Dream Sequence Putts: 'Well, on 18, I kind of said to myself in my head, and I've said it to my coach a few times—that's the putt you've seen guys hole,' he will say if the putt goes in. 'O'Meara is the one that comes to mind. That in my mind might have been a bit longer, but that's the one guys hole to win it. You've seen the read. You know it goes a bit right-to-left. I just told myself to go with instinct. Just put it out there and hit it. Show everyone how much you want it. This is the one. And then 10 was—I mean, it's amazing, because I wasn't comfortable with my shot into 10. I had to just kind of feather a 6-iron a bit. I was excited, so I knew I was going to hit it hard and I needed to hit it soft.

'But the putt on 10, I could hardly see the green in the darkness. Really, I was struggling to read it. So I gave Steve the call over. I didn't get him to read too many putts, because I felt like I was reading good. I said, "Do you think it's just more than a cup?" He said, "It's at least two cups. It's going to break more than you think." I said, "I'm good with that." He was my eyes on that putt. I needed the line because I wasn't comfortable looking down there. It was really dark and he's seen a lot of putts at this golf course. Somehow, he might have been able to recall that one. I knew it was a fast putt, so I said, "I'm going to hit it to kind of go in the front edge, so I want a line for that." And he said it's at least two cups. So an unbelievable read. It started on line and managed to hang in and go in the left half. An amazing feeling.'

The Sportsmanship: 'You know, Angel is a great man,' Scott will say if the putt goes in. 'I think he's a gentleman. To give me a thumbs up is very nice. With limited abilities to converse, you know, we would consider each other friends and have a lot of respect for each other. It's an incredible camaraderie between all of us out here.

'His chip on the first playoff hole was just beautiful, and unlucky not to go in. That must have gone right over the edge of the hole. My heart was about to stop. I was standing at the side of the green thinking, is this it, really? But you know, managed to skid one up there myself and knock it in.

AMEN

'And then he hits a beautiful putt on 10, as well. Those things can just as easily go in as go out. I had a similar putt to him on 10 earlier today, and it was a perfect putt he hit.'

If the putt goes in, Adam Scott will salute his first and most important coach: 'I think that's really fair that you say that, because although Greg was an inspiration to me and a hero as a player, my dad was the one who was always there with me right from the get-go. He's a professional golfer himself, and my mum is a good golfer, too. But Dad coached me until I was nineteen years old. And when we were there down by the 10th green, it was great to see him. He said, "It doesn't get any better than this," which is true. You know, he's the biggest influence on me. He was a great role model for me as a kid, as I think back on it, and the way he balanced everything for me so that I just kind of made my own way as a golfer.

'Really, he did an incredible job of just letting me be who I am and letting my game develop. Not standing in my way at times and pushing me when I needed to be pushed. He's an amazing man. Obviously he's always been there for me, the good times and the bad. He was at the Open last year and he was as positive as anyone. I'm sure he was gutted inside, but it's nice that I'm able to kind of reward him with this one today while he was here.' Grinning, he adds: 'He only comes to those two events.'

Scott can recall every last detail of his round. Every yardage. Every club. Every roll of the Titleist Pro V1. Tell us about the first hole: 'I hit a driver off 1 and it went left. I had to punch a 6-iron from about 145 yards, chip and run a 7-iron and two-putted for bogey.' The second: 'I hit a 3-wood in the right rough. I laid up with a 6-iron, hit a lob-wedge on the fringe and two-putted for par.' The seventh: 'I hit a 3-wood and a 9-iron just short, and chipped with a sand wedge to a couple of feet, and one-putted.' Remarkable. How can you remember all this? The 13th: 'I hit a driver and a 7-iron. I chipped with a sand wedge from the bank to a couple of feet and one-putted.' The 17th: 'I hit a driver, 9-iron, I don't know how far that was, 25 feet maybe, 30 feet, 25 feet and two-putted for par.' The 18th: 'I hit a driver, 8-iron to 25 feet and made it.' And then you stood on the balcony of the Augusta National clubhouse and picked at your cuticles and gave the rain your thousand-yard stare and pondered what the fates might have in store.

'Playoff holes,' says Scott.

'What happened?'

·· ● ··

If the Putt Goes In . . . 'Holing that putt is a massive moment for him but also for all Australian golfers,' Leishman will say. 'Whether it be me, playing with him in the last round at Augusta, or Jase Day, who had a chance to win, or a ten-year-old watching it at home on TV in Australia, every one of us was wanting him to win. I went back to our house and turned on the TV, and it was right when he was holing that putt on 10. I think I fist-pumped again in front of the TV, jumping up and down. My wife, Audrey, was laughing at me—it was funny because I don't even really fist-pump my own putts. Then all of a sudden I'm acting like an idiot in front of the TV for Scotty. Mum and Dad were there, and my wife and son.

'To get that monkey off the backs of all Australian golfers is enormous. The monkey of, when are you going to win the Masters? We've done it. Massive. Whoever it was, I probably would have felt the same thing because it was such a big moment for Australia. It's going to be great at next year's Masters because we're not going to get asked that question again. When is an Australian going to win? Why haven't you won? All this. Now we're going to get asked, can you back it up? This is probably the only thing we've never won. Cadel Evans won the Tour de France a couple of years ago, got that out of the way. We've won the America's Cup. We've won all the biggest events—Wimbledon, the US Open tennis, all the big tennis events. The US Masters was always there as the only one we hadn't really done.

'I think having three of us in contention helped. If it had've been just one Australian in the lead, it would have been a lot harder to deal with that pressure. Not that the country puts pressure on you, but you know everyone is willing you on so hard. When you know it's going to be the first time, it's a lot of pressure. For Scotty to get that up-and-down on 18 in the first playoff hole, and then to birdie 10 in the dark, that was unbelievable. Scotty deserved it but Cabrera put up an unbelievably good fight.'

·· ● ··

If the Putt Goes In . . . Peter Thomson will be watching from his lounge chair in Melbourne. 'I

AMEN

was a bit anxious about it,' he will say. 'Never in my career did I hole two putts like he did on the 18th and second playoff hole. The whole game was different in my time. You played for two putts. That was the sensible way to go. You putted it dead if you could and then you tapped it in. As far as holing it went, that was asking for trouble. I felt awe. Awe that somebody could hole a putt like that. I was thrilled to see it go in for him. I wanted him to get out of it with a win otherwise for the rest of his life, people would be pointing their fingers and saying he can't win. This proved all that was bunkum. My wife was holding my hand, I think, at the time.'

·· ● ··

If the Putt Goes In . . . Bruce Crampton will be on the phone to his wife. 'She's out in California, and I told her I was actually trembling,' he will say. 'The adrenaline was flowing. It wasn't highs and lows for any particular player. I just knew what it meant to them and that hopefully was history was about to be made. I didn't wait to see the presentation ceremony, but my wife had high praise for Adam and the way he handled it. I hope he goes on now and wins more.

'I've been told that Greg Norman had some very nice things to say about me. That's the second time he's done that. Apparently he made some comment about the fact that Adam and Jason gave him credit for inspiring him to do what they have done. And then he mentioned Bruce Crampton was the one that inspired him. That's something to be very proud of.

'I've only met Adam once, on the first tee at Royal Sydney in 2006 when Golf Australia asked me to be their guest for the 50th anniversary of my victory. I have long been an admirer. I think he probably has the best swing in golf by modern standards. There's only one thing wrong with it. And that is that it isn't mine. As soon as the Masters was over, I came upstairs and took the Australian flag I had, and I put it on my flagpole. It will fly all week in honour of Adam and his fantastic victory.'

·· ● ··

If the Putt Goes In . . . Jack Newton, as always, will go straight to the point: 'The 100-pound gorilla is off his back.'

·· ● ··

If the Putt Goes In . . . the only leader board that matters, the leader board after The Back Nine On a Sunday, will read:

-9 Adam Scott (Australia) 69–72–69–69★
-9 Angel Cabrera (Argentina) 71–69–69–70
-7 Jason Day (Australia) 70–68–73–70
-5 Marc Leishman (Australia) 66–73–72–72
-5 Tiger Woods (USA) 70–73–70–70
-4 Thorbjorn Olesen (Denmark) 78–70–68–68
-4 Brandt Snedeker (USA) 70–70–69–75
-3 Sergio Garcia (Spain) 66–76–73–70
-3 Matt Kuchar (USA) 68–75–69–73
-3 Lee Westwood (England) 70–71–73–71
★ Adam Scott wins on second playoff hole.

··●··

If the Putt Goes In . . . Phil Scott will beam for all his living days. 'I still have people coming up to me every day,' he will say a couple of months later. 'I'm still smiling. I see the little photo on the phone every day and think about it. One is that photo where he's holding his arms up with the jacket on when it is dark. It's almost like a halo photo. It's a beautiful photo. The other one is just after he has holed the putt. I still look at them and think it's unbelievable. I guess one of the things I keep thinking is, gee, he can go back there forever. I'm sure it has sunk in but it's still just a great feeling. I hope I reflect on that forever, to be honest.

'I guess one of the things I am really chuffed about is how people here have been. It's been something that has really been embraced in Australia. I think that's really cool. I guess he has got to a point of maturity and maybe status. If your background has been that you are not outlandish, people will respect your opinion a bit. I think there's a bit of that with Ad. He hasn't been the guy making silly comments or being nasty. I think when he does say something it's usually something he does have a good think about.

'When I try to strip away the parental bias, I get the significance of it. It was something we hadn't done here in sport in our country. For twenty years it was always Greg. I get why people think it's special and I guess it is, in that sense. I am sure now it will open the door. Jason has knocked on the door twice at Augusta and he's a kid. Leishman will come out of that tournament thinking I was at the top of that leader board all week, and I did not fold.

He has got to walk out with great confidence. We see that generally—one of our guys does well and they all do well.'

••●••

If the Putt Goes In . . . 'I have tried on the jacket,' Phil Scott will admit. 'It mightn't be a perfect fit, but who cares? I have my photo of that. I'm not going to play Augusta until I can play with Ad. That will be something special for me. I will peg it up with Adam and we can play Augusta together while he is the Masters champion.'

••●••

All this will happen if the putt goes in. Miss, and we'll be coming back tomorrow.

It's the prettiest putt he ever hit.

Clink.

ACKNOWLEDGEMENTS

Gratitude to Adam Scott and all the golfers who make themselves readily available to the media at the Masters. Many thanks to Phil Scott, Brad Malone, Greg Norman, Peter Thomson, Jack Newton, Bruce Crampton, Ian Baker-Finch, Craig Parry, Col Swatton, Charlie Epps, Paul Leishman and Marc Leishman. As well as our own interviews, material for this book was obtained from press conferences during the Masters, plus tournaments in the US, Europe and Australia. The article 'No Jacket Required' cited on p. 27 appears on Greg Norman's personal website <www.shark.com>. Adam Scott's remarks about broomstick putters on pp. 85–6 are from an interview with *The Sunday Times*' chief sports writer David Walsh.

ABOUT THE AUTHORS

WILL SWANTON has been an award-winning sports writer for 15 years. He's written for *The Australian, The Sydney Morning Herald, The Sun-Herald, The Daily Telegraph* and *The Sunday Telegraph* newspapers. He has received the Australian Sports Commission's award for the best contribution to the coverage of sport by an individual. He's been published by Australian Associated Press, Reuters, Agence-France Press, *Wisden, The Guardian, International Herald Tribune, South China Morning Post* and *The New York Times*. His photographs have been published by Reuters and *The Australian*. He's twice featured in *Best Australian Sports-Writing* compilations and has travelled extensively to report on the Olympic Games, Paralympic Games, Commonwealth Games, Australia's Test and World Cup cricket campaigns, Test and State of Origin rugby league, Bledisloe Cup rugby, all four major tennis championships and the Association of Surfing Professionals world championship tour. His other books are: *Ian Thorpe: Early Days, Some Day, Murderball, The Mighty Mullygrubber Malone, A Better Life* (with Craig Hamilton) and *The Slams*.

BRENT READ is a sports writer for *The Australian* newspaper. He has covered golf both in Australia and overseas, as well as other major events such as the Olympic Games. This is his first book.